A FISTFUL OF FIVERS

FROM MICHELSTADT TO
UPMINSTER

MARTYN WILLIAM IFFLAND

Edited with an Introduction and Annotations

By

Claire Adele Lansley

Published in 2025

The right of Martyn William Iffland to be identified as the author of this work and Claire Adele Lansley as the author of editing, annotation, Introduction and Later Years has been asserted in accordance with the Copyrights, Designs and Patents Act 1988

A CIP catalogue record for this book is available from the British Library.

DEDICATION

This book is dedicated to our parents
Martyn and Brenda Iffland
who raised us and who were by each other's sides
for their entire adult lives

ACKNOWLEDGMENTS

With grateful thanks to my husband Charles for the very many hours spent helping me with editing and proofreading. His expertise has been invaluable. Also to my mother Brenda, sister Jan and brother Peter for their support in publishing this work.

CONTENTS

ABOUT THE AUTHOR

MARTYN WILLIAM IFFLAND

Martyn Iffland was born in 1932, the son of a German teacher, Johannes Iffland and a British woman, Ruth Goldstein, who became a German citizen through marriage. Ruth's father was Jewish, and although he had renounced his heritage, Ruth was subject to anti-Semitism while living in Germany in the run-up to the Second World War. She was forced to flee to her parents' home in Upminster, Essex, England, taking her two children with her. Her husband did not go with them, promising to follow on later, but he never did. He divorced Ruth under Nazi Law and Martyn saw his father only briefly once thereafter, when he was twenty-one. From the age of seven, he was raised by his deeply religious Christian Missionary grandparents.

He left school at the age of 16 with no qualifications and was given employment by a local Land Surveyor. Mr Story took Martyn under his wing and trained him to become a Land Surveyor. The work was hard and involved long periods away from home, working both in the UK and the Middle East. However, he forged a successful career, establishing his own firm, *Iffland and Associates*, with his younger brother Edgar in 1970.

He first met his wife when she was 15 and he was 18. Five years later they were married and they went on to have three children. Their first child Claire was born in India while he was working away from home on an 18-month contract. Their second daughter Janet was born back in the UK, and the memoir ends with the birth of their third child Peter.

Martyn became a Director of the Guild of Incorporated Surveyors and of the UK Land and Hydrographic Survey Association Ltd. He was a founder member of The Survey Association of which he became first a Committee Chairman, then Vice President and finally President from 1994-1997. He retired in 1997, aged 65.

In retirement he lived in the same house that he and his wife had purchased in 1970, just a stone's throw from his grandparents' home. He passed away there in 2022.

ABOUT THE EDITOR

CLAIRE LANSLEY

Claire Lansley is the eldest daughter of Martyn and Brenda Iffland. She was born in India in 1958. Her father had been asked to undertake an 18-month survey contract for his employer, and as his wife was already pregnant, arrangements were made to allow her to go with him.

From her return to the UK aged 9 months, Claire grew up in Cranham, Essex, moving with her parents at the age of 11 to Courtenay Gardens, Upminster. She went to school locally and then to the London Hospital Medical College in Whitechapel, East London. This was the place where her great-grandfather John Goldstein and her uncle, John Iffland, had both trained before her. She qualified as a doctor in 1982. Having chosen a career in Obstetrics and Gynaecology, she was awarded the MRCOG by examination in 1989 and the FRCOG in 2001. She worked as a Consultant Obstetrician and Gynaecologist from 1995 up to her retirement in 2016.

She married her husband Charles in 1989 and has two children, Charlotte and William, and two grandchildren, Rupert and Merryn.

INTRODUCTION

by
Claire Lansley

This memoir was written by my father over several years in the mid-2000s when he was in his seventies. He intended it to be read by his family after his death and did not allow anyone to read it while he was still alive, with the exception of his eldest grandson Henry. The book covers the first 32 years of his life.

It starts with his birth in Hanau am Main in Germany and details his family background. Most of his first four years were spent with his parents and grandparents in Salonika in Greece. The family then returned to Michelstadt in Germany where he spent the next three very happy years. These years had a profound influence on him, which lasted for the rest of his life. This small town was a place that he loved.

His happiness was broken when, at the age of just seven, he and his mother were forced to leave Germany and flee to England because of the rise of anti-Semitism and impending war. He had to leave his German father, whom he only saw once again as an adult. He maintained his links with his German family as much as he could and would visit whenever possible. The only problem was that he no longer spoke the language, as he had naturally been required to speak only English after he arrived in England in 1939.

His story continues through the War and into his teenage years when, at the age of eighteen, he first met my mother. At that time he was working as an apprentice Land Surveyor in Upminster where he lived and he went on to make a successful career in Land and Engineering Survey.

At the age of 23 he married my mother in 1955, a marriage which lasted 66 years until his death at the age of 89 in 2022. Their early years of marriage were marked by prolonged absences from home caused by his work and the requirement for him to travel extensively around Great Britain and also abroad to Iraq and India. I was born in India during one such contract. Luckily, my mother was able to travel abroad with him for the first time.

Thereafter, my sister Janet and brother Peter were born, and the book ends with my brother's birth in 1964.

The title of the book comes from a constant refrain of my father's. He would never ask for any gift for himself, but was always very generous to others. Whenever he was asked what he would like for Christmas or a birthday, he would reply "a fistful of fivers". He probably got the expression from "A Fistful of Dollars", used for the 1964 Clint Eastwood film of the same name.[1]

---

[1] A 'fistful of dollars' literally means a collection of notes that will fit into the palm of one's hand. Figuratively it suggests a considerable sum of money, perhaps enough to make a notable difference or to satisfy a financial need. The expression can be used when someone has unexpectedly won or received a large sum of money.

Martyn and Brenda Iffland June 1995 © CA Lansley

1
MY ARRIVAL

Wilhelm Martin, the second son of Johannes Iffland and Ruth Minna (born Goldstein), came into this world alone with his mother on the 2nd of July 1932 at the home of Wilhelm and Luise Jung: Vor der Kinzigbrücke11, Hanau am Main, Germany.

The place where I was born © Google Maps

Vor der Kinzigbrücke11, Hanau am Main. The family Jung lived in the first-floor apartment © CA Lansley

My brother Johannes Franz had been born in Salonika, Greece, on the 22nd of June 1931.

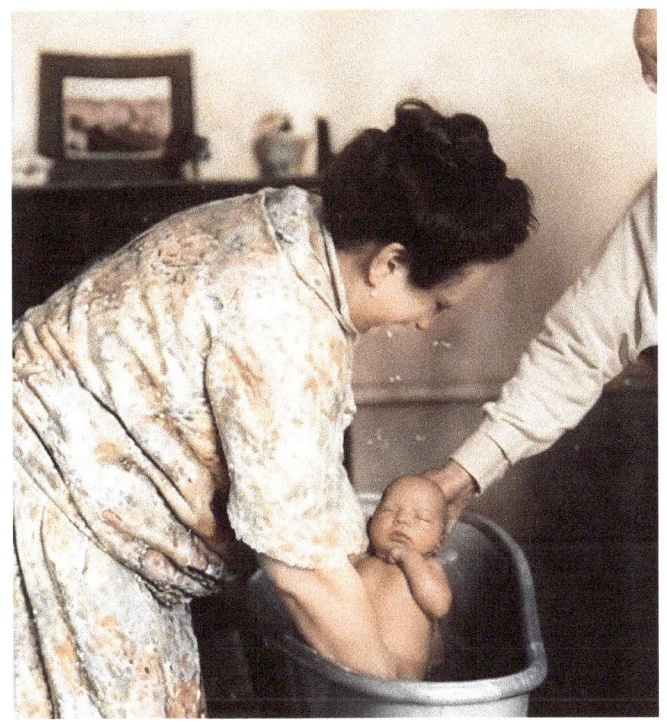

July 1931 Baby brother Johannes Franz with grandparents
'Noni' and 'Opa' (Octavia and Johannes 'John' Goldstein)
© CA Lansley

The Johannes Iffland family, comprising Mother, Father and baby Johannes, travelled from Salonika to Germany for the summer of 1932, pending my birth. My parents had been invited to stay with Wilhelm Jung (married to Luise Iffland, sister of my paternal grandfather, Andreas). They were accommodated in Hanau until I was born. In recognition of this, my parents named me after Herr Jung. I was to be called Wilhelm, and also Martin, after my mother's brother. The official birth notification recorded the normal German form, whereas my mother wanted my name to be as her brother was known as 'Martyn'. It may well have been that my parents, knowing that I was soon to be born, wanted me to be a German citizen.

My birth certificate © CA Lansley

2
MY FAMILY BACKGROUND

The photograph below shows my godfather, Wilhelm Iffland, and his wife, Luise (second row from the back), at the marriage of Wilhelm Iffland to Emmy Alles in 1923. The groom was my great-uncle, my paternal grandfather Andreas' brother. My great-grandmother (Hanauer Oma) is sitting on the bride's right, and my grandparents are standing, second row back, behind the bride and groom. Second row from the back, Father, at the age of twenty, is the fifth person counting from the right. Onkel Franz stands behind his left shoulder.

Photograph of the 1923 Iffland wedding © CA Lansley

Mother was the daughter of Dr Johannes Leopold Goldstein MRCS, LRCP and Octavia Nina (eighth child born to Dr John and Ada Reynalds).

The Reynalds' family home in Bristol © CA Lansley

Grandfather Johannes Goldstein ('Opa') came to England from Germany as an eighteen-year-old in July 1891 after being converted to Christianity in Danzig, where he had been born to Jewish parents. He first had to learn English and achieve the required level of education needed to study Medicine. On the 11th of October 1897, he registered as a Medical Student at the London Hospital, University of London, and qualified as MRCS, LRCP on the 27th of April 1903. Subsequently, he joined the London Christian organisation, the Mildmay Mission to the Jews, and was trained as a Medical Missionary. He married Octavia Nina Reynalds ('Noni'), a Christian worker, on the 15th of July

1903, and together they served the Mission in many parts of Europe, Morocco and Greece.

Letter heading from the Mildmay Mission to the Jews
© CA Lansley

The photograph below was taken in Tangier in 1911, where the family was posted, together with Miss Fison, Uncle Martyn, my mother and my grandmother Octavia. Miss Fison was a fellow Missionary worker who also acted as a governess for the children.

Tangier 1911 Miss Fison, Martyn, Ruth and Octavia
© CA Lansley

So much of my information about the early years is gleaned from the back pages of my grandfather's Bible, where he chronicled the family's important events. His exceptional life is given in his autobiography *All The Doors Were Opened* (1950).[2]

_____

[2] Goldstein, John (1950). *All The Doors Were Opened.* London: The Messianic Testimony.

Father (Johannes Iffland), perhaps in 1926 © CA Lansley

Father was an expatriate school teacher who had left Germany in about 1925 to teach at the German School in Salonika. Having recently read Mark Mazower's 'Salonika City Of Ghosts',[3] I was surprised that Father would have chosen to go to Salonika in view of the serious turmoil over so many years in that city. On the other hand, as a Medical Missionary, I can see why my grandfather was posted there on the 1st of November 1923, bringing with him my

---

[3] Mazower, Mark (2005). *Salonica City of Ghosts: Christians, Muslims And Jews.* Harper Perennial

grandmother, and my mother as a sixteen-year-old girl. Her siblings, Uncle Martyn and Aunt Margaret, had been left to continue their schooling with Christian friends, the family Pastor Urbschat, in Neuwegersleben, Germany. In Greece, there was serious deprivation among the Jewish community and no doubt scope for physical healing while attempting to convert Jews to Christianity.

Father met my mother no doubt through the German community, and they became engaged and married at the German Embassy, Salonika, on the 14th of June 1930.

My parents, Johannes Iffland and Ruth Goldstein. I think Mother was showing off her engagement ring!
© CA Lansley

The Mediterranean Palace Hotel © CA Lansley

The Wedding Reception was held at the Mediterranean Palace Hotel on the seafront near the White Tower. A second wedding ceremony was then held at the Evangelische Kirchengemeinde, Beerfelden, on the 12th of July 1930, when they also celebrated the wedding of Onkel Karl, my father's brother, and Tante Marie.

Wedding Invitation © CA Lansley

Auszug aus dem Trauregister

der evang. **Pfarrei** Beerfelden

Jahr 193o **Seite** 23 **Nr.** 21

Bräutigam:	Name, Vornamen, Familienstand, Religion, Beruf, Alter (falls eingetragen, Geburtsdatum), Wohnort usw. Iffland, Johannes, Lehrer zu Saloniki geb.am 2o.11.19o2 in Erbach
	Trautag, Trauort 12. Juli 193o Beerfelden
Braut:	Geburtsname, Vornamen, Familienstand, Religion, Beruf, Alter (falls eingetragen, Geburtsdatum), Wohnort usw. Goldstein, Ruth Minna geb. 28.4.19o7 in London
Eltern des Bräutigams:	Name (Geburtsname der Mutter), Vornamen, Beruf, Wohnort, Angabe ob verstorben usw. Andreas Iffland, Diamantschleifer zu Hetzbach
Eltern der Braut:	Name (Geburtsname der Mutter), Vornamen, Beruf, Wohnort, Angabe ob verstorben usw. Dr. John Goldstein, Missionsarzt wohnhaft zu Saloniki
Bemerkung:	z. B. Angaben über Trauzeugen, die als Verwandte der Brautleute erkennbar sind, usw. Urbschat, Pfarrer zu Groß-Leiningen begleitet von Pfarrer Knodt, Beerfelden

Beerfelden , den 31.8. 19 95

Tgb. Nr.
DM 10. -(zehn)

Ev. Pfarramt West 64743 Beerfelden i.Ode.
Pfarrer S. Aras
Marktplatz 10
64743 Beerfelden

Form. 186 W. Lang & Co., Friedberg

Evang. Pfarramt:

A. Gitjahr

Copy of the Marriage Register held in Beerfelden,
Germany © CA Lansley

3
MY FIRST FOUR YEARS IN SALONIKA, GREECE

My parents lived in Salonika where Johannes was born and returned there following my birth in Germany.

Brother Johannes with Noni in Salonika 1931
© CA Lansley

Me and Johannes © CA Lansley

Left to right: Johannes, my mother Ruth, Aunt Dadit, me,
my father Johannes © CA Lansley

Memories of life in Greece 1932-1936 are very vague and largely recalled from photographs taken during this period and the frequent references made to Salonika and the many friends there, by my mother and my grandparents. From all I subsequently learnt, this was a happy time, in spite of accidents such as when, obviously not under proper supervision, I fell into an adjacent open lime pit where builders were working. I have a letter from my father written on the 11th of June 1953 when he mentions this incident. He enclosed some of my hair from then, bleached, even more so than my already blonde hair at that time.

One vague memory was of a visit to the Nuns, Sisters Marie and Hedwig, at their home in Kavala, where chocolate, sea and my squint featured prominently.

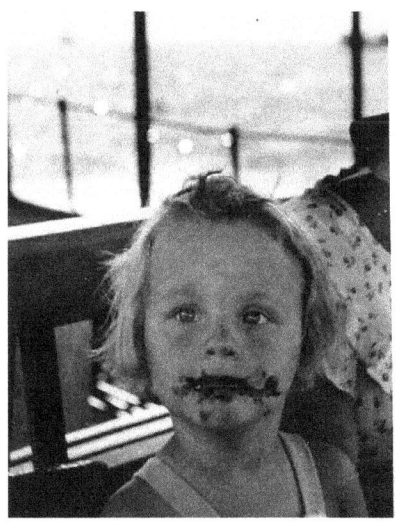

Me in Kavala, Greece © CA Lansley

In 1936, due to the advent of Hitler, as my mother was half-Jewish, she was debarred from attending the German Club in Salonika. With the noises of war in Europe, my family returned to Germany in 1936. This might also have been influenced by the fact that my Uncle Martyn had died of meningitis in Salonika on the 28th of November 1935, exactly five years after he had been involved in a serious road accident in Berlin. In that accident, he sustained four skull fractures yet also survived an episode of meningitis two years later.

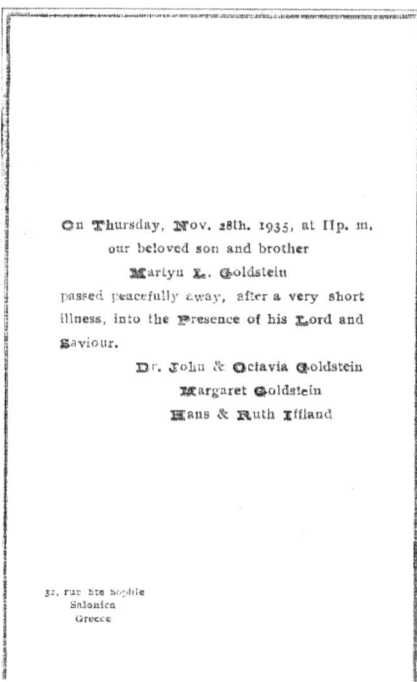

On Thursday, Nov. 28th. 1935, at 11p. m., our beloved son and brother
Martyn L. Goldstein
passed peacefully away, after a very short illness, into the Presence of his Lord and Saviour.

Dr. John & Octavia Goldstein
Margaret Goldstein
Hans & Ruth Iffland

32, rue Ste Sophie
Salonica
Greece

Death Announcement of Martyn Goldstein © CA Lansley

16

Mother, Johannes and me © CA Lansley

Whether our return in 1936 was under official instruction from the German Consulate or because of the realisation that the rumblings involving Adolf Hitler and his Brownshirts were becoming louder, I do not know. Neither have I any recollection of the journey home to Germany, but of course it would have been by train.

My grandfather had earlier been expelled by the Authorities from Greece for 'religious propaganda' and had returned to England.

4
MICHELSTADT, GERMANY

My early positive recollections are of our home at 67 Wald Strasse, in the house built by Wilhelm Rodenhaeuser in 1903, in the beautiful little walled medieval town of Michelstadt, in the heart of the Odenwald. Father had rented a first-floor flat in Wald Strasse from Herr Rodenhaeuser after he had been appointed to a teaching post at the Volkschule in Michelstadt in March 1937.

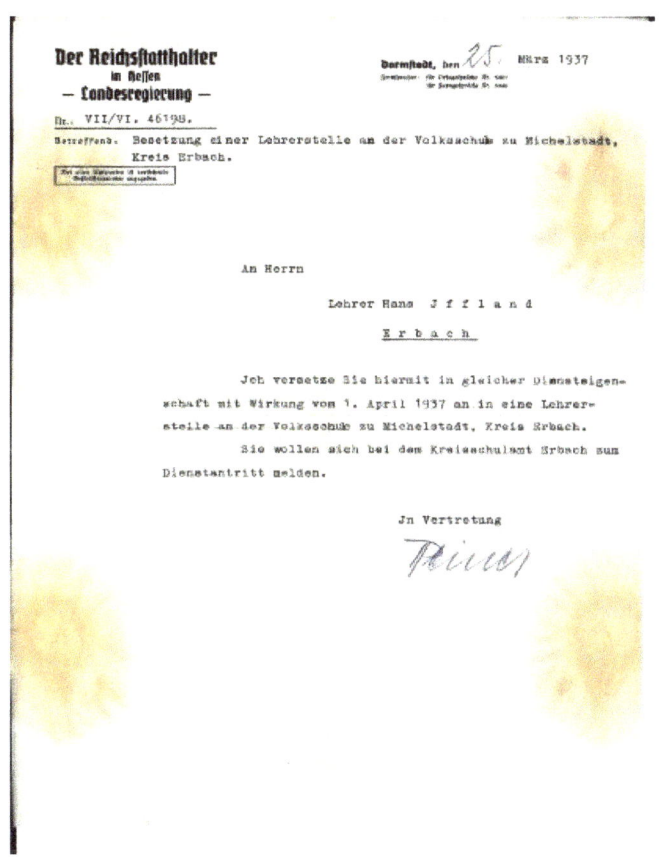

Suddenly, he was taken seriously ill with peritonitis, and Mother, having always been shielded by her parents or by my father, felt very isolated, with two small boys in a very difficult environment. He had an operation which was successful, but he was unable to work for some time, and as small-town teachers were very poorly paid, life was a struggle for them.

All this time, anti-Semitism was becoming more serious and Jewish cemeteries and properties were being vandalised. Mother had received anonymous hate letters and finally, when she became pregnant, no doctor would accept her. So it was thought best for us to leave Germany for England as soon as possible, where my maternal grandfather, a doctor, could look after us and the soon-to-be-born baby. I have only recently discovered these details while reading old letters.

However, my brother John and I, in 'Lederhosen' and with an Aryan father, were unaware of all of this and did not find ourselves singled out. We clicked our heels and saluted the Führer, whose portrait had to be displayed in every home. John had to join the Hitler Jugend[4] while I just tagged along.

Life was regimented. From records dated the 15th of January 1937, which I have from Mother, we were given a form of ration book where it was noted from whom we were allowed to buy certain essential goods: the 'Haushaltsnachweis'.

---

[4] The Hitler Youth

Ration Registration dated the 15th of January 1937

© CA Lansley

Kundenliste

für Speck, Schmalz und Talg					für andere Fette				
Nr. der Kunden-liste	Eingetragen		Gelöscht		Nr. der Kunden-liste	Eingetragen		Gelöscht	
	bei Firma (Unterschrift oder Stempel)	am	bei Firma (Unterschrift oder Stempel)	am		bei Firma (Unterschrift oder Stempel)	am	bei Firma (Unterschrift oder Stempel)	am
257.	Johann Weber Metzgerei Michelstadt-Odw.				58	Adam Körber Kolonialwaren Michelstadt i/Odenw.			

Ration Registration with Johann Weber Metzgerei (butcher) and Adam Koerber Kolonialwaren (grocer).

© CA Lansley

There was also the Eintopf Tag (One Pot or Stew Day) when everyone would be expected to cook the same meal. I can clearly remember us being visited by an official to ensure we were complying. My recollection was of a helmeted man, but that was likely to have been a policeman as they then all wore spiked helmets. That immediately brings to mind my fear of these large men with spiked helmets, or so they appeared to a little boy.

As a way of 'encouraging' saving, Hitler had decided that each family should be enabled to be a car owner, after all, he had built these wonderful new autobahns. To publicise this, in the square in front of the Erbacher Schloss, probably in 1938, were lined up for inspection, perhaps half a dozen Volkswagen cars. It was like a feast day, everyone could own such a car, and our parents took us to marvel at what the Führer was doing for the people. But of course one had to pay instalments each month, I believe, rather like a rent book, but I cannot be sure. Unfortunately few people ever saw anything for their money.

This Volkswagen display is forever linked in my memory with the spike-helmeted policemen who on that day patrolled between the cars and perhaps spoke sharply to us, and I recall Mother saying that, in contrast, how wonderful the English policemen were.

67 Wald Strasse circa 1903 © CA Lansley

The house in Wald Strasse seemed vast. We occupied this end of the first floor. We explored the open framed sheds where the winter logs were kept dry, to the large cellar where every tenant had their allotted space to store their goods (and large jars of home- made 'sauerkraut' with its own distinctive smell, but wonderful to eat!). Each tenant of the Rodenhaeuser flats had a small garden off a large grassed meadow. Along one side was a row of mulberry trees and at the entrance to our plot Mother had planted nasturtiums. She always loved flowers. Although it was huge in my memory, on returning in 1953, I had great difficulty in identifying the place because it appeared so much smaller than my childhood memory.

Johannes and me at the top end of the garden, probably in 1937 © CA Lansley

Herr Rodenhaeuser was a dear old gentleman with a moustache and cropped hair. From time to time we would go up to his flat at the top of the house and play with his 'inflation money'; billions of Marks not worth the paper on which they were printed. He, in common with so many people, lost so much in the Great Depression. Unfortunately, we here, and in so many parts of the world, are now (in 2009) entering this same 'Inflation/Deflation' period once again and world leaders do not appear to know the way out.

Promises and the changes all could see, in terms of economic recovery after so many years of unemployment, led the mass of working people to support Hitler's 'Third Reich', even when many could see that war was coming, as rabid anti-Semitism continued to sweep the country. I recall all our unhappiness when Herr Rodenhaeuser died in 1938. As I was not allowed to attend, I watched the funeral procession from our first-floor flat.

Herr Rodenhaeuser with his wife and granddaughter
© CA Lansley

For a very young boy Michelstadt was an exciting place. John at the age of seven had to go to school whilst as a 'Mummy's boy' I stayed home. I envied John his 'Erste Schultag Tüte', a large colourful conical twist of cardboard holding all sorts of wonderful sweet things, almost as tall as the child. Something to remember and no doubt a small bribe to get the child to attend willingly. I never received one. For a short time I did sit at the back of the class to familiarize myself with some more discipline, but my lamentations meant that, as I was underage, I quickly returned to my mother.

Johannes with his Erste Schultag Tüte © CA Lansley

Carnival time is also very clear in my memories of this lovely old town. John and I had no costumes to join in the parade, but being a deft needlewoman, Mother made large colourful bobbles from wool and sewed them onto our pyjamas. We were so proud.

For every town, even small ones, Hitler had ordered athletic and swimming facilities to be constructed, no doubt with the aim of producing healthy young Germans to fight for him as he planned the dominance of Europe. Michelstadt boasted an Olympic-sized pool set on the slope overlooking the town surrounded by the woods of the Odenwald. Father took us there regularly in the summer and on the grassed surrounds was gymnastic equipment such as parallel bars and rings. Our uncles Franz and Willi were both 'county' level athletes and were anxious that John and I should follow their example. Not for me. John was always the stronger, but hanging by the arms from those rings at seven years of age and trying to swing between the parallel bars was beyond me.

The pool also had a high-water chute which John would happily climb and slide down, but for me it was frightening. At one time Father said he would buy me a large ice cream if I climbed to the top and descended. He said he would wait at the bottom and catch me. Yes, I was persuaded to climb and descend, but he failed to catch me. I thought I was drowning, but of course only for an instant. I never went underwater again after that fright until I was twelve years old, when a kindly Mr Adamsbaum, co-worker at the Mildmay Mission to the Jews, took London East End boys camping at Mersea, Essex. There I learnt to swim.

From a child's perspective, life was good or the recollections largely were. After Father was called up to attend summer 'Lager' (in spite of his bad eyesight), which I now realise was preparation for the mobilisation of civilians, on his return to us he came with baskets of soft fruit, strawberries, raspberries, and currants, much to all our delight. It was on his return that I recall Father wanted John and I to box each other. This I refused to do, but under pressure agreed to wrestle.

There was also one Christmas that I recall well. In the normal way Christmas was celebrated on 'Heiligabend,' the twenty-fourth of December, and we were not allowed into the room where the decorated Christmas tree stood until the early evening, candles alight and presents around its base. There was also always a beautiful tree in the square outside the Rathaus (The Town Hall). Eventually, bursting with excitement and anticipation, John and I were called in, but where were our parents? A large framed box, rather like a flimsy television without its screen and draped to the floor stood in front of us, and from it strange voices asked if we had been good. I was utterly petrified and I think I cried loudly asking for our parents. John was rather more stoical, but we were both very alarmed. We made so much noise that our parents emerged from behind it to pacify us. They had secretly made the 'Caspar Puppen Theater' (Punch and Judy) as a special surprise for us thinking we would be delighted, but I was so afraid I hated it.

This same Christmas we both received marzipan mice. I hid mine somewhere in the bedroom and managed never to eat it. I still do not like marzipan!

Annually a country celebration called 'Schlachtfest' was held, when pigs were slaughtered in the main street by the local butcher. I remember hearing the squealing, then the silence. It was frightening for John and me. Then every part of the animal was processed as all the villagers joined in, cooking meat, preparing sausages and making soup. Nothing was wasted. This was all with much beer, wine and merrymaking. For those young men who had not witnessed this ceremony before, such as John and I, we were scooped up in our uncle's arms and given a moustache with the fresh pig's blood, much to Mother's disapproval. Onkel Franz, who had lifted me up, had such a rough chin that I can almost feel it today.

*Mother with Johannes on her lap. I am wearing a white
T-shirt in the back row. © CA Lansley*

In 1938 we went on a visit to Frankfurt Flughafen where
we saw a Graf Zeppelin.[5] These photographs, which
reminded me of our visit in 1938, were photographed by me
from a television programme (on the 11th of February 2010)

---

[5] The last flight of the Graf Zeppelin was from Friedrichshafen to
Frankfurt on the 18th of June 1937 where it remained on display until it
was broken up by the Luftwaffe in March 1940.

which recorded the epic circumnavigation of the globe by Graf Zeppelin.[6]

We were allowed to go onboard and see where the captain would stand at the controls.

© *In the public domain*

The pod was formed under the airship's forward belly. We also saw the accommodation units which stretched back inside the airship. Everywhere was exposed aluminium

---

[6] The TV programme that my father saw was of the documentary 'Around the World by Zeppelin' by the Dutch director Ditteke Mensink using 1929 film footage. This was first aired on BBC Four on Thursday the 11th of February 2010. The circumnavigation took place in 1929, going from New York, Friedrichshafen, Moscow, Tokyo, Los Angeles, and back to New York. This fascinating documentary can be seen on YouTube at https://www.youtube.com/watch?v=p0sPTxA01BQ.

framing and between it was a narrow metal walkway, along which I really was afraid to walk! (even more so than when Father wanted me to go down the water chute at the swimming baths.) In all it was a very interesting day.

We were also helped very occasionally by our paternal grandfather Andreas, who ran the family diamond cutting business in Hetzbach and was also a licensed Jaeger (authorised hunter to cull the deer in the forest). On one particular occasion, he brought us some fresh venison. I remember how delicious it was but have never in later years found any that tasted as good. Their family home and business had a water wheel providing power which was a major attraction for all the youngsters and young cousins. Franz, John, and I tried, and occasionally succeeded, in netting small freshwater crayfish which at that time were abundant. We were only allowed in grandfather's workshop under strict supervision, with the noise of the great lathes slapping away, turning the grinding wheels.

Johannes and me © CA Lansley

5
GRANDFATHER ANDREAS IFFLAND'S FAMILY

On a visit to Michelstadt (May 2006), I read a book about early Erbach and its inhabitants and the surrounding villages. This interested me further regarding the life of my grandfather Andreas Iffland who was born in Bruchköbel, Hanau on the 21st of May 1877 and his wife Eleonore born in Erbach on the 18th of December 1880. After marrying in 1901 they struggled to raise four boys (Johannes, Karl, Wilhelm 'Willi' and Franz), the eldest of whom was Father.

Grandfather was initially employed in a diamond cutting business, 'Goldee' in Lauersberg. In 1925, having received training in the jewellery business by family members in Frankfurt, Grandfather bought the house at Erbacher Strasse 70, Hetzbach. The house had previously been used as a cloth dyeing works. A friend Herr Uhrig and his son Otto made a major contribution to the project of repairing and making the building structurally suitable to house the family and also to accommodate the electro-mechanical lathes and grinding tables, all of which were harnessed to the stream flowing behind the house. Water from the 'Bach' (stream) was diverted to power the lathes for cutting and polishing the rough diamonds.

In due course, (I believe about 1925) Father left Germany and travelled to Salonika in Greece to teach there in the German School. I have no idea what prompted him to leave a close knit village family to travel abroad, but his sons, John, Edgar, and I all had the 'wanderlust'; in that John, after qualifying as a doctor at the London Hospital (where both his maternal grandfather and subsequently his niece qualified as doctors) was posted to various places abroad with the Royal Army Medical Corps, while both Edgar and I travelled as Land Surveyors in many countries.

Onkel Willi married Emmi Karg on the 19th of April 1926 in Darmstadt. They then ran the Post (an old Post Inn) near Hetzbach Railway Station, a stone's throw from the parents' home. Their children, Otto, Anneliese and Ruth, all had reasonable space in the large house.

Onkel Willi and Tante Emmi 19th April 1926 © CA Lansley

In 1930 my parents came from Greece to celebrate Onkel Karl and Tante Marie's wedding in the Beerfelden Church and there they also renewed their own vows; those they had made earlier in the month at the German Embassy in Salonika. I have a photograph of this day, below, with Father wearing his familiar bow tie.

Johannes and Ruth Iffland July 1930 © CA Lansley

Father's brothers Karl and Franz had entered the diamond cutting business with their father. The business was known as 'Andreas Iffland & Söhne Diamantschleiferei' (this from Grandfather Andreas' letter heading). They shared the restructured house in Erbacher Strasse with their parents, their wives and their growing families. Onkel Karl and his wife Marie occupied the house's basement. They eventually had six children: Franz, Lore, Karl, Trude, Helga and

Hedwig and all shared the cramped basement, suffering the noise of the lathes far more than the other family members.

My impression was that Karl was largely supervising the workroom and Franz was working with his father dealing with the purchase of the raw stones and selling the finished articles, but I am unsure of the details. Grandfather Andreas and Grandmother Eleonore occupied the ground floor, which included the workroom, the one shared kitchen and a small office, while Franz, who had married Sophie Karg (sister of Emmi) on the 1st of September 1935, shared the upper floor with his wife, and their two children, Franz and Rosemary.

The rough diamonds were held in a claw that was abraded against the wheel in front of each man, a very slow, painstaking process, but with extreme precision needed to ensure the highest quality cutting. Each night the floor was very carefully swept in case any small chip might be lost. The uncut stones came mainly from Antwerp, the European centre, and the majority were from Jewish dealers.

The Diamond Workshop © CA Lansley

During the war it was impossible for Grandfather to deal with Jews, and then after the war, the Jews who were rebuilding their trade would not, unsurprisingly, deal with Grandfather. The business closed. Grandmother Eleonore died during the war in June 1943. Grandfather Andreas died on the 6th of October 1946.

Eleonore and Andreas Iffland © CA Lansley

6
BEFORE THE WAR

In the summers of 1937 and 1938 we briefly visited our grandparents at 24 Ingrebourne Gardens, Upminster. They had settled there after leaving Greece, Grandfather having been refused re-admission, except for a short stay in Salonika in November 1935 when he received permission to see their dying son Martyn.

Mother's passport © CA Lansley

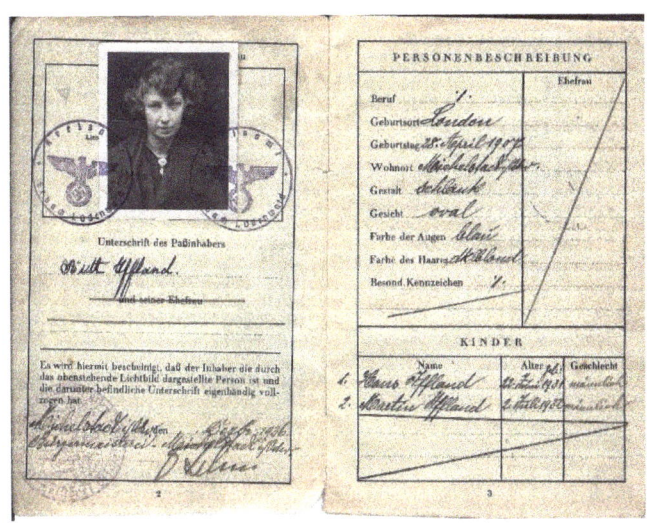

Mother's passport © CA Lansley

On our visit to Upminster our grandparents hired a small bicycle for us to enjoy, and both John and I learnt to balance, with a little help from Mother.

Ingrebourne Gardens, Upminster 1937 © CA Lansley

Ingrebourne Gardens, Upminster 1937 © CA Lansley

There were nineteen fruit trees in the garden, wonderful for boys to climb, but at that time too early for the fruit.

John and me at Southend on Sea © CA Lansley

Although I have no recollection of those early journeys to England, it must have been by train with many changes at the borders, then the ferry, followed by train to Victoria Station, London and down to the Underground, to be met at Upminster Station by our grandparents. Today, one has little concept of how difficult foreign travel was, especially with young children. The journeys back and forth to Michelstadt are lost in the past; only that final journey to England in 1939 is seared in my memory.

Once back in Michelstadt my memory largely goes blank. I believe the same pattern of life continued, playing with friends, enjoying the huge decorated fir tree in the square outside the Rathaus at Christmas, having 'Steinpflasters', spicy Christmas biscuits shaped like cobblestones. There were regular trips to Hanau to visit Tante Luise and play with our 'cousin' Rudi where Tante Luise and Onkel Wilhelm would make us very welcome.

Mother, Johannes and me with Rudi circa 1936
© CA Lansley

Michelstadt Rathaus (Town Hall) © CA Lansley

But the reality of life was more serious. In an effort to prove our Aryan background, we were obliged to produce an 'Ahnen Pass', a family history record based on Church and other entries. Mother wrote to her mother in England for more information as to her ancestry, which was traced to the 17th century, but one could not disguise Grandfather's Jewish origins. All this time anti-Semitism was becoming worse even though we could show Father's ancestry to 1735, as an Aryan German. The Jewish cemetery was desecrated and properties vandalised.

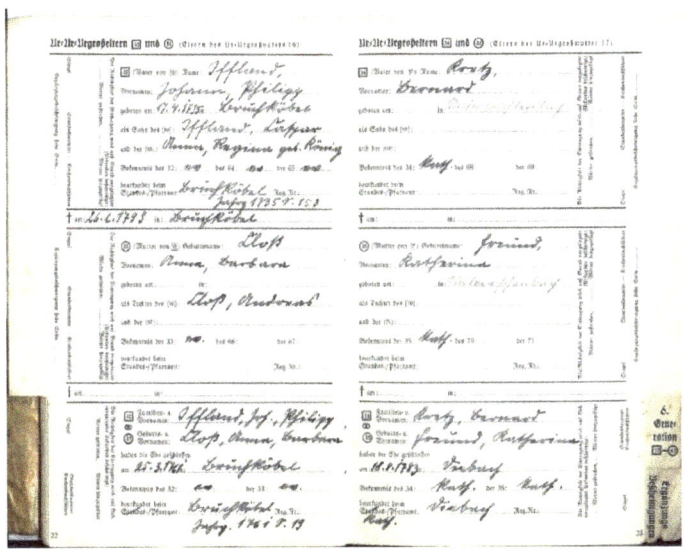

Father's Family Tree © CA Lansley

Recently I read that Mother was receiving anonymous hate letters and, finally, when she became pregnant, no doctor would attend her. It was therefore decided best for us to leave Germany for England, where Grandfather, as a doctor, could look after us and the baby soon to be born. Eventually we were given permission to leave Germany, but Father had to stay.

Leaving Father behind is seared in my memory and brings tears to my eyes whenever I think of it, even today as an old man. Father had to force my fingers from his hand as I could not bear to be parted and he promised to join us soon, but with the War declared in that September he never came to us. Mother was then seven months pregnant. Brother Edgar never saw his father.

Recently I was told that having a half-Jewish wife in the 1940s threatened my father's State employment as a teacher. He divorced my mother under Nazi law, believing that Germany would win and we would never meet again. I believe that long-term separation was also a factor.

In July 1939 we travelled to Hanau. There, we said our goodbyes and took the train which would eventually bring us to London again. However, we were held up by the German border police at Aachen for three days and only the intervention of the British Consul enabled us to leave.

7
ENGLAND AND THE WAR

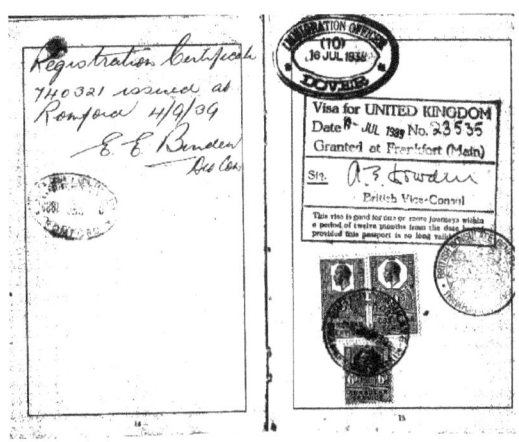

Our Visa for the United Kingdom © CA Lansley

The previous exhausting journeys to England had been easier than the present. Now the railway carriages and boats were crammed, as all who could were leaving Germany and Europe generally, with war imminent. I remember we were all standing in the crowded train from Dover to Victoria, London, when one English gentleman got up and gave his seat to Mother. No one had done so before. We travelled to Upminster by the District Line underground train and, apart from the welcome we always received from our grandparents, my memory goes blank.

24 Ingrebourne Gardens, Upminster © CA Lansley

I just remember being in a long back garden full of fruit trees, and a tall silver birch tree in the front garden, which still remains, but two others have been taken down.

24 Ingrebourne Gardens, Upminster (by silver birch and yellow van) © CA Lansley

John and me circa 1939 © CA Lansley

Once in wartime England our names took on the anglicised form of Martyn William and my brother, John Francis.

In July, John and I were given a belated joint birthday and we each received a small toy plane which made us extremely happy, as did the bananas which we had not eaten for some time. Another food we tasted was the cereal still available today, 'Rice Crispies', known to us as 'Snap, Crackle and Pop'. We liked listening to the sound when milk was added!

Then on the 10th of September 1939, as John and I were playing, we were called to come upstairs, where in the small back study Mother had just given birth to a new brother,

Edgar, weighing in at over ten pounds. We dutifully kissed this pink bundle and were then allowed back to our play.

Although it meant little to us at first, suddenly the threat and Declaration of War with Germany on 3rd September meant learning to wear a gas mask, issued to all. We also obtained a special gas-proof cot in which Edgar could lie in the event of an attack.

Fire Wardens had been mobilised to ensure that light-proof curtains were hung at all windows to minimise enemy aircraft identifying our location; air raid warning sirens would sound with a wavering tone eventually followed by the 'all clear', a continuous note. Practice runs were held and I remember the warning siren sounding in the daytime, and we had to run indoors, draw the curtains, put on our gas masks, which I hated (I thought I would die, unable to breathe) and we all sat round the dining room table with the lights out!

These two young boys brought to England in their 'Lederhosen', clicking their heels and saying 'Heil Hitler' had to be re-educated without delay and taught to speak English. My brother John was attacked by boys further up Ingrebourne Gardens and so we were quickly togged-out in English clothes at Roomes' Men's Store, a little way up from the present store.

My grandparents were active members of the Brethren; they were Lutheran in outlook and worshipped at the small

'Old Chapel' in St. Mary's Lane opposite the Abraham's family windmill. Each Sunday, we would attend Sunday school and were invited to join in their social circle. One recollection was of attending probably my first children's party, and to my consternation was expected to play 'Postman's Knock'.

There were flashes of wonderful times when our Aunt Margaret, affectionately known as 'Dadit' (John's very early attempt to pronounce her name which stuck for life) came to see us from her work as a State Registered Nurse, and at one point foolishly promising that she would take us to Roomes' Stores to buy us each a dressing up suit; John as the Cowboy and I as the Indian. What bliss when eventually she took us to keep her promise.

Soon after war was declared, Mother was advised that being married to a German National she was considered an 'Enemy Alien'. She had to register and was not permitted to live within a certain number of miles of the coast, even though we were some twenty or more miles inland.

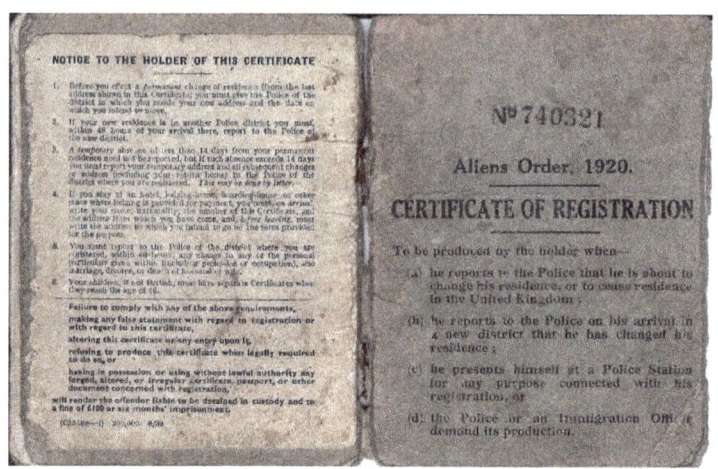

NOTICE TO THE HOLDER OF THIS CERTIFICATE

Nº 740321

Aliens Order, 1920.

CERTIFICATE OF REGISTRATION

Mother's Certificate of Registration in the UK
© CA Lansley

From Upminster we then had to go inland, but where? The only place we could find accommodation was at a flat 'Manuka', connected to the Mildmay Mission to the Jews, Central Hall, Philpot Street, Whitechapel, just behind the London Hospital. There we went by the kindness of the Mission's Chairman, the Rev. Harcourt Samuel.

John and I were sent to a Junior School just around the corner in Varden Street but due to the frequent air-raid warnings we were in and out of shelters most of the time. A remaining memory of the school was of being made to drink those small bottles of milk issued to children, which I hated.

Aunt Margaret had come to join us at 'Manuka' and as the air raids grew more severe each night, we all spent most nights in the large basement. The bombing grew much worse and one night we all crossed over to Whitechapel Underground Station and joined scores of people sleeping on the platform. The train running current had been switched off. The proximity of so many bodies on the platform was too much and we eventually returned to the basement of the Mission, where one young man played his accordion to keep us entertained.

During one surprise raid, Mother was hit on the head by a piece of shrapnel, probably from an anti-aircraft shell fragment. Fortunately, it was not too serious. A bomb left a crater at the road junction a few yards from the Mission in Philpot Street. When in the daytime an explosion rocked the Mission, Mother shouted to us to get under the table and threw herself over the pram containing Edgar. Fortunately no one was injured. The docks could be seen in flames and the City of London was severely damaged.

One night Mother and Aunt Margaret could take no more and perhaps foolishly decided to try and get back to Upminster, so with Edgar in the pram, John and I walking alongside, we set off. It was dark and cold with searchlights criss-crossing the night sky, the drone of bombers overhead, the noise of the Bofors ack-ack guns, a very frightening experience. Mother was at her wits' end. We walked and walked for what seemed an eternity when suddenly a door opened and a lady called out to come in out of the street and shelter in her house. This we gratefully did and were given breakfast the next morning. What wonderful people the

Eastenders were. We had walked from Whitechapel to this home in Ilford in the middle of a blitz. The next morning we managed to eventually take the bus to Upminster. However, we were not in the clear as we were still not allowed to remain in Upminster despite Grandfather's pleas to the authorities.

Through Christian contacts we were given temporary accommodation with a middle-aged couple living in Uxbridge. I regret that I cannot even recall their name. It was a difficult time for all. Air raids were continuing every night and we would have to leave the house and go into the 'Anderson' shelter dug in the garden, probably designed to accommodate four people, now needing to cope with six, Aunt Margaret having made alternative arrangements. I am sure that we were not particularly well-behaved boys. The lady of the house wore a wig which she took off when coming into the shelter, quite an unusual sight for youngsters and perhaps we found it amusing or frightening, but our stay was relatively short!

Our next move was to the elegant home of the Misses Fison at Westcott, near Dorking, a very pleasant place to live. Margaret Fison of the industrial family Fison had agreed for us all to stay in their lovely home until more permanent accommodation could be found. She had been a fellow Missionary worker and joined my grandparents in Tangier, Morocco in 1910 where she also acted as a governess for Mother and Aunt Margaret, who had been named after her. It was during this stay at Westcott that I caught whooping cough and, once again, thought that I was dying.

Aunt Margaret was unmarried and at this time developed a relationship with an American soldier stationed nearby. Before long, complaints from the neighbours to the Misses Fison ensured that we were quickly on the move once again. This was in early 1942.

Application had been made to Surrey County Council for housing and we were happy to accept accommodation at 47 Poole Road, West Ewell, which was ideal. John and I attended a nearby school.

My tenth birthday was memorable. I was given a tent which was the pinnacle of my dreams and John and I slept in it in the garden on the 2nd of July 1942.

As children we did not appreciate the situation, but Aunt Margaret and her American friend took a flat in the centre of Epsom where on the 20th of October 1941 she gave birth to a girl, Lois, named after her good American friend Lois Riess from Salonika. The birth caused extreme consternation in our ultra-conservative family and a serious rift remained for very many years. The baby's father was in due course repatriated to America and Aunt Margaret, to her credit, would not have the child adopted. A great love was generated between mother and daughter all her life.

It is very difficult to recall and comment on the way our lives developed. School for me in West Ewell was a very difficult time and to my shame I was too frightened even to ask to leave the classroom to go to the lavatory and consequently wetted myself at my desk. By this time my command of reading must have been better than the command of my bladder for I recall enjoying the book 'The Story of Nelson.'[7] I do not know just how long we stayed in West Ewell but my next recollection was of being back in Upminster in about 1944 and starting at a small private school 'Minster House' which occupied two adjacent private houses in Corbets Tey Road at the foot of the hill leading to the 'Huntsman and Hounds' public house, where opposite there was operating an old smithy. With the wartime shortage of fuel, I remember buses going up the hill past the school looking odd, towing trailers filled with large bags of gas as diesel was scarce.[8] With time I became more settled thanks to the kindness of the headmaster Mr George Hartley

---

[7] The book my father read is most likely *The Story of Nelson* from *The Children's Heroes Series* by Edmund Frances Sellar with pictures by Monro S. Orr. The edition was first published in 1906 but was reprinted in the 1930s by Thomas Nelson and T.C. & E.C. Jack Ltd.

[8] During and after WWII the supply of oil was restricted. London buses pulled trailers carrying wood/coal gas generators. They fed the petrol engines with a mix of hydrogen, carbon monoxide and methane obtained by burning wood or coal with limited air, allowing the engines to work at less than half of their nominal power. Fifteen million wood/coal gas generators were sold in Europe in the 1940s. Here is a link to a photo of the kind of bus in London my father would have seen, trailing a wood/coal gas generator: https://www.ianvisits.co.uk/articles/londons-ww2-%20experiment-with-coal-powered-buses-54446/

who even lent me his own bicycle to travel the distance from Corbets Tey to home in Ingrebourne Gardens.

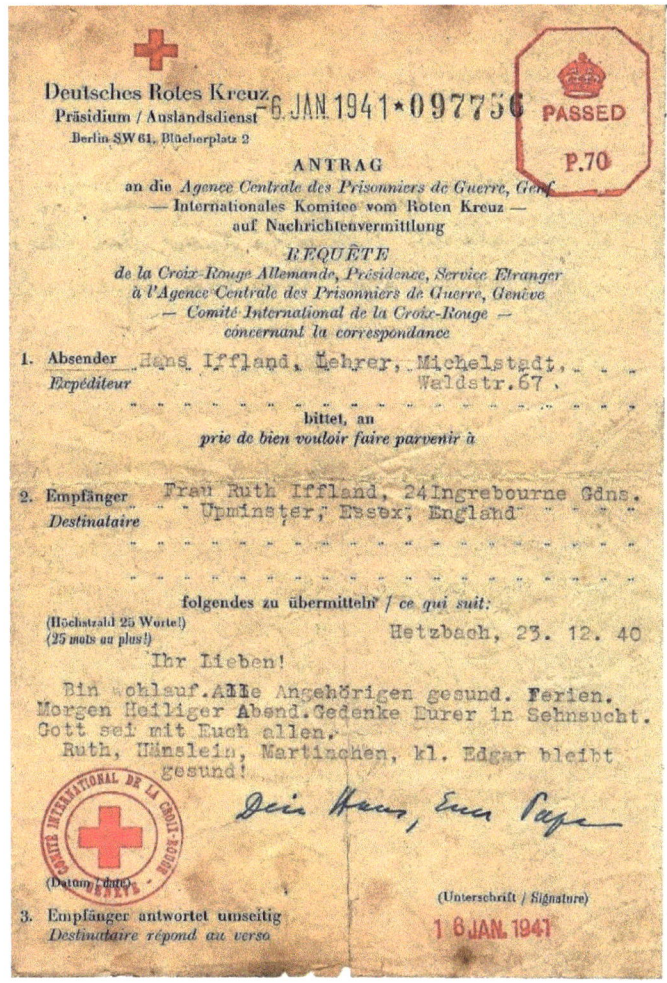

The one letter received from Father, sent the day before Christmas Eve, received in January 1941 © CA Lansley

Left to right: Onkel Wilhelm, Tante Luise, Tante Emmi,
Onkel Willi in Army uniform, Rudi as a young boy, Hanauer
Oma, and my father in 1943. I was given this photograph
after the War. © CA Lansley

Throughout the war we prayed for our father, and Mother
made desperate efforts to communicate through the Red

Cross. We received just a few words at Christmastime in 1941, on a form on which your reply could be made. Then silence and we did not know if he was still alive.

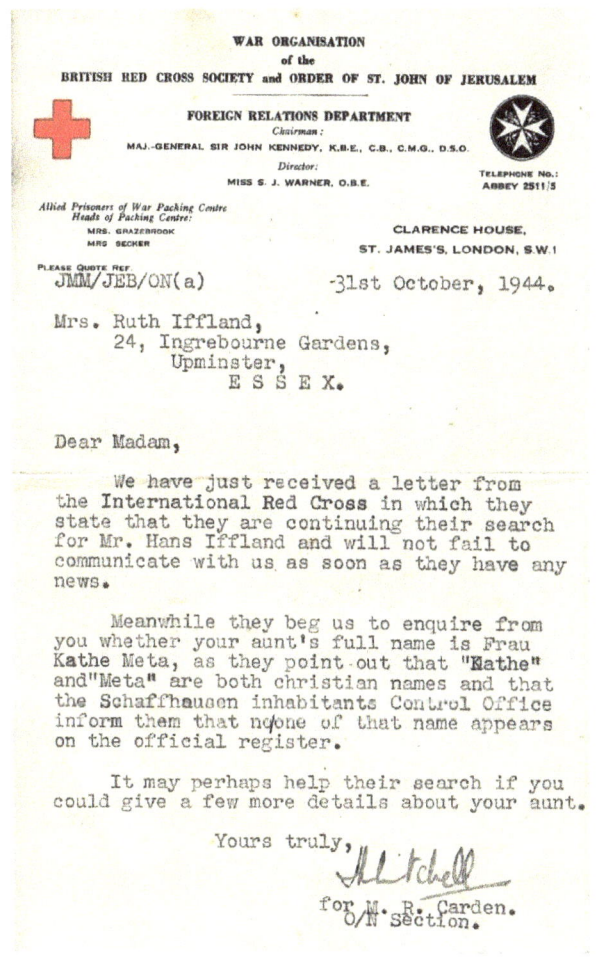

WAR ORGANISATION
of the
BRITISH RED CROSS SOCIETY and ORDER OF ST. JOHN OF JERUSALEM

FOREIGN RELATIONS DEPARTMENT
Chairman :
MAJ.-GENERAL SIR JOHN KENNEDY, K.B.E., C.B., C.M.G., D.S.O.

Director :
MISS S. J. WARNER, O.B.E.

TELEPHONE No.:
ABBEY 2511/5

Allied Prisoners of War Packing Centre
Heads of Packing Centre:
MRS. GRAZEBROOK
MRS SECKER

CLARENCE HOUSE,
ST. JAMES'S, LONDON, S.W.1

PLEASE QUOTE REF.
JMM/JEB/ON(a)   -31st October, 1944.

Mrs. Ruth Iffland,
    24, Ingrebourne Gardens,
        Upminster,
            E S S E X.

Dear Madam,

        We have just received a letter from
the International Red Cross in which they
state that they are continuing their search
for Mr. Hans Iffland and will not fail to
communicate with us as soon as they have any
news.

        Meanwhile they beg us to enquire from
you whether your aunt's full name is Frau
Kathe Meta, as they point out that "Kathe"
and "Meta" are both christian names and that
the Schaffhausen inhabitants Control Office
inform them that noone of that name appears
on the official register.

        It may perhaps help their search if you
could give a few more details about your aunt.

        Yours truly,

        Mitchell

        for M. R. Carden.
            O/N section.

Mother's search for her husband through the Red Cross
1944 © CA Lansley

61

We sang a little hymn in Spanish every day to keep Father in our minds, but I do not know why as we knew the English translation.

'El me sostendrá, El me sostendrá, Pues que sus me Armarse, El me sostendrá…' *'He will hold him fast. He will hold him fast because My Saviour loves him so. He will hold him fast.'*

This is probably a jumbled recollection, but we were asking God to look after our father.

The German Red Cross sent Mother a letter dated the 22nd of November 1944 stating that on the 1st of May 1944, Father had divorced my mother and on the 26th of July 1944, he had married Hedwig Breitwieser.

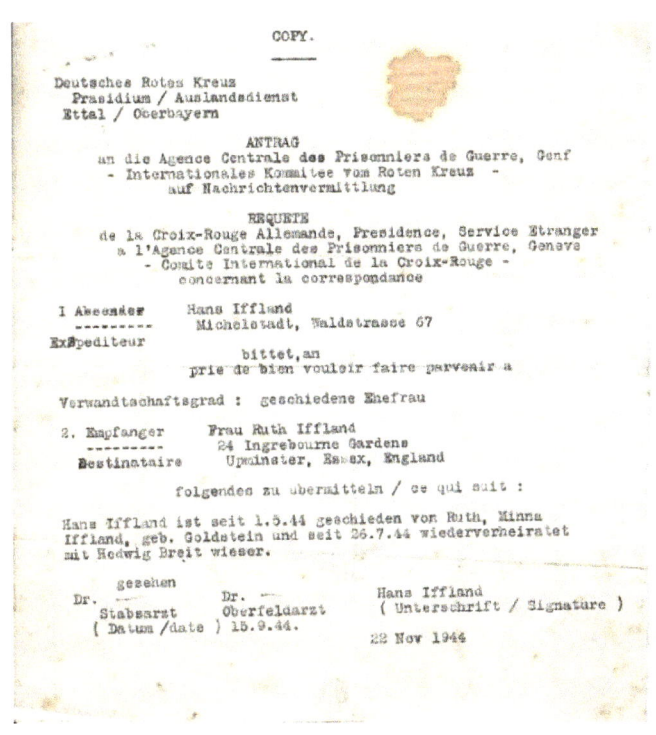

Letter from the German Red Cross 1944 © CA Lansley

I remember Mother's utter devastation, standing in the kitchen at No. 24, unbelieving, screaming her pain and hurt. We never prayed for him again.

In the post-war years Nazi law was discredited and eventually, after many years and with the help of our wonderful 'cousin' Rudi, her claim to a small part of Father's pension was realised, meagre as it was.

A brief mention should be made of VE Day 1945. Victory in Europe brought to an end the terrible slaughter on the battlefields but also a respite from the deadly bombings on civilian targets which both sides had suffered. However, the war against the Japanese continued in the Far East until the atomic bomb on Hiroshima finally brought the war to an end.

Each village and town in Britain celebrated VE Day (Victory in Europe) with street parties, finding and making goodies from the meagre rations of the time. Tables were laid down the middle of the street, and everyone joined in the happiness of the war's end. Behind my friend Alan's parents' home in Ingrebourne Gardens, once a miniature golf course, we all built a huge bonfire, collecting everything combustible from helpful and enthusiastic neighbours. This was May, and we boys could hardly contain our impatience to light the bonfire, but it was well after 9 pm before it was dark enough. We had the good fortune that one of the neighbours was a senior Fire Warden who brought a large lump of phosphorus which, when thrown onto the blazing bonfire, lit up the whole of the surrounding area!

8
TEENAGER

After the war, Mother had applied to the Home Office for her children and herself to be re-categorised under the British Nationality and Status of Aliens Act, as she had lost her English citizenship on marrying my father. We were granted a Certificate of Naturalisation EZ.30 on the 20th of July 1945.

Oath of Allegiance.

I, *Ruth Minna Offland*

swear by Almighty God that I will be faithful and bear true allegiance to His Majesty King George the Sixth, His Heirs and Successors, according to law.

(Signature) *R. Offland*

Sworn and subscribed this **17** day of **July** 1945, before me.

(Signature) *A W Hole*

Justice of the Peace for *The County of Essex*

~~A Commissioner for Oaths.~~

Address { *110 Castellan Avenue* *Romford Essex* }

Unless otherwise indicated hereon, if the Oath of Allegiance is not taken within one calendar month after the date of this Certificate, the Certificate shall not take effect.

Mother's Oath of Allegiance to the Crown 1945
© *CA Lansley*

BRITISH NATIONALITY AND STATUS OF ALIENS ACT, 1914

Certificate of Naturalization granted to a woman
who was at birth a British subject and is married to a subject
of a State at war with His Majesty

Whereas • Ruth Minna Iffland

who was at birth a British subject and is the wife of an alien who is a subject of a
State at war with His Majesty, has made a declaration that she desires to resume
British nationality and has applied to one of His Majesty's Principal Secretaries of
State for a Certificate of Naturalization alleging with respect to herself the particulars
set out below :

And whereas the Secretary of State is satisfied that it is desirable that the
said Ruth Minna Iffland

be permitted to resume British nationality and that such a certificate may properly
be granted :

And whereas the said Ruth Minna Iffland
has also applied for the inclusion in accordance with sub-section (I) of section five
of the said Act of the names of her children born before the date of this Certificate
and being minor s , and the Secretary of State is satisfied that the names
of her children as hereinafter set out, may properly be included :

Now, therefore, in pursuance of the powers conferred on him by the said
Act, the Secretary of State grants to the said

Ruth Minna Iffland

this Certificate of Naturalization, and declares that upon taking the Oath of
Allegiance within the time and in the manner required by the regulations made in
that behalf she shall, subject to the provisions of the said Act, be entitled to all
political and other rights, powers and privileges, and be subject to all obligations,
duties and liabilities to which a natural-born British subject is entitled or subject,
and have to all intents and purposes the status of a natural-born British subject.

And the Secretary of State further declares that this Certificate extends to
the following minor children Johannes Franz – born 22nd June, 1931 and
of the said Ruth Minna Iffland. /Wilhelm Martin – born 2nd July, 1932.

In witness whereof I have hereto subscribed my name this 28th day of

June, 1945.

Under Secretary of State.

HOME OFFICE,
LONDON.

PARTICULARS RELATING TO APPLICANT.

Full Name	Ruth Minna IFFLAND.
Address	24, Ingrebourne Gardens, Upminster, Essex.
Trade or occupation	Of no occupation.
Place and date of birth	Tottenham. London. 28th April, 1907.
Nationality	German (by marriage).
Name of husband	Johannes IFFLAND.
Names and nationality of parents	John Leopold and Octavia Nina GOLDSTEIN (British by naturalization). *(For Oath see overleaf.)*

Certificate of Naturalisation for Mother, John and Me 1945
© CA Lansley

My time from 1944 to 1949, when I left school was, to say the least, inauspicious. My brother John had taken an entry examination for Palmer's School, Grays, and made very good progress, whereas on starting school I had great difficulty even in telling the time and understanding the limited education on offer. Once again, in the early years, I was in and out of the air raid shelter which had been dug into the bank opposite our school.

My 'achievements' as such did not amount to anything much. On one Minster House School Sports day I managed to gain two bronze second-place medals for events 4 and 17, though I have no recollection of what these events were! And a silver First for the High Jump at 5'4". In July 1948, I was awarded a First in Class No. 38 (based on age) at the Cranham & North Ockendon Annual Show, for a pencil drawing of Upminster Windmill. I only wish that I could have been more attentive to my schoolbooks, for I had a lot to catch up later.

From our first meetings as children, a bond had formed between Alan Lazell, who lived at No. 19 Ingrebourne Gardens, and me, as we lived almost opposite at No. 24. We spent many hours in each other's company, playing on the disused miniature golf course behind Alan's house. At the east end of the course was a small pond with bulrushes growing, sticklebacks and all sorts of pond life of interest to us. At this time, British troops were stationed in Ingrebourne Gardens as invasion preparation plans were underway.

Troops with their vehicles, Bren Gun Carriers[9] and lorries were parked in the street outside our homes. The vehicles were having a thick waterproof compound stuck all around their headlights, or wherever water could be a problem, as they mobilised. We had built camps out of sticks and reeds, constructed a tree platform and used old discarded hot or cold water tanks to 'sail' on the pond. Unfortunately, we constantly had problems with leaks as well as stability, as they were prone to tipping over regularly! From friendly soldiers, we managed to scrounge enough of their compound to plug most of the water tanks' inlet/outlet pipes and bravely cast off from the shore, only to find the water pressure stronger than our plugs, however much we persevered, and consequently often arrived home wet and reeking of the sweetish, rotting reeds. No 'Health and Safety' prohibitions then!

In June of 1944, we had to keep an ear open for the drone of the German 'doodlebug' flying bombs. We knew that as long as we could hear the drone of the jet, as it followed the Thames heading for London, all was well for us. It was only when it cut out that the missile was a peril as it plunged. The larger rocket which dropped without warning from the sky gave no chance of escape, but thankfully relatively few of these landed in our vicinity.

---

[9] The British Universal Carrier—often incorrectly referred to as the 'Bren Gun Carrier'—was a WWII vehicle used by every Allied army in every theatre. Picture at https://warfarehistorynetwork.com/wwii-vehicles-the-british-universal-or-bren-gun-carrier/

Another friend of very long standing, John Greenfield, recalls that he, as a youngster, approached 'our territory' and tried to pick up some plums which had fallen to the pavement from a neighbour's overhanging tree, to be told by me that those were 'our' plums and he, coming from Hall Lane, had no right to them! Needless to say, John is a long-lasting friend with whom Alan and I have, and continue to share, happy times and memories.

Another school friend was Neville Thompson. We were both cyclists. I had been given a new red Raleigh Sports No. 636179P with a Brooks B17 narrow champion saddle for Christmas in 1948. Neville was already a member of a cycling club and used to compete in 'Time Trials.' We planned to make a tour of Devon and Cornwall in August 1949 using Youth Hostels en route. (I still have the 1949 YHA Handbook, which listed all the Hostels in England and Wales.) In February we had made a long weekend ride to Dovercourt and Aldebrough and the surrounding area, staying with Neville's aunt, and found the going not too bad, in spite of a strong head wind on our return, but of course a trip to Land's End would be a different challenge.

Neville Thompson (above) and me (below) 1949
© CA Lansley

Neville at Plymouth, the Hoe, tough going uphill,
Lostwithiel Youth Hostel and waves at Land's End 1949
© CA Lansley

We joined the Youth Hostels Association and the Cyclists' Touring Club, (of which Grandfather was a member in the late 1890s; I still have his CTC lapel badge). We planned the route, staying at a different hostel each night so the targets we set ourselves had to be met.

We set out from Upminster on Saturday the 6th of August 1949 and headed southwest to Holmbury St. Mary. The next day we headed to Winchester, then to Cerne Abbas, Witherage, Torquay, Plymouth, Lostwithiel, Phillack, Penzance and we finally reached Land's End on the 14th. My recollection was that we were lucky with the weather as my diary records no rain. At the time my grandparents were holidaying in Bristol (my grandmother's childhood home) so from the most south-west tip of England we rode on to Gidleigh, then Witheridge again and to Bristol where we successfully met up in the city centre.

After this we headed to Marlborough, Buckingham, and then on to our goal, the British Grand Prix at Silverstone on Saturday 20th August, with its noise, smell of fuel and fantastic drivers such as Ascari. We also saw a demonstration motorcycle (Broughton Special?) where the rider lay horizontally instead of astride his huge machine. Neville's aunt's home backed onto the racetrack and for the last day he went there. I then cycled back to Upminster alone on the 21st of August, arriving at 3.13 p.m. after having come down the hill at Childerditch Common too fast and instead of joining the T junction lane, I overshot and ended up in a ditch. Luckily no damage to self (except pride!) or my bike. My average speed for the day was 14.6 mph (I had a cyclometer fitted).

From my school days I had also made a good friend of Peter McInery, a tall, broad chap who was the initiator of much fun spent at his home in Corbets Tey Road and at the Upminster Recreation grounds, full of mischief and mechanically minded. After school, he had entered the Ford Motor Company in the Trade School, his father being a relatively senior Ford employee. Peter was interested in boxing and had invited me to join him to watch some of the 1948 Olympic Boxing at The White City Stadium. I must confess that while it was interesting to have been there, boxing as such did not appeal to me at all, always being afraid of physical pain.

Aunt Margaret had moved to Bartestree and invited me and Peter to cycle (some considerable distance) to see her in the summer. With parental approval, Peter and I set out on planned stops en route, where Peter's parents had contacts. I am not certain whether they were relatives but they were thought to be kindly people who would put us up overnight.

We made the first leg of our journey and were welcomed and put in a double bed, after insisting that we each had baths! It was a restless night and I am sure that we were given the oldest possible sheets, but to our alarm, in twisting and turning in bed, Peter and I managed to make significant tears in our sheets. The next morning when the lady of the house saw the damage we had done, she was extremely cross and she insisted that we must repair the sheet with needle and thread, which we dejectedly did, to the best of our ability! I am unsure whether she gave us breakfast but I suspect that it was frugal. Then off once more on our bikes for the last leg to see my aunt.

Coming into contact with so many mechanically minded youngsters, some of whom owned motorcycles, it was not long before Peter's father agreed to buy him one and he proudly showed me his gleaming new 250 AJS. On the 13th of November 1949, Peter went on a club run with his new Ford friends and the next thing I heard was that in spite of wearing a crash helmet, which was not compulsory at this time, he had crashed and died near Thaxted.

It was a very difficult loss to bear, only made easier by the friendship of Alan and Geoffrey Davies, the brother of Dylys (who was to become Alan's wife in 1957) and Neville. Peter's death and the subsequent cremation were to me a landmark. As we had all been members of the Crusaders Union Bible Class, we attended the ceremony at the City of London Crematorium and my horror at the process of cremation I retain today.

Peter McInery, Margaret and me © CA Lansley

As we had been playing cricket on the old miniature golf course for some time, it was decided to play opposing teams and in 1949 we established the Ingrebourne Cricket Club. I still have the bat given to me by Mother on my fifteenth birthday.

My 15th birthday present © CA Lansley

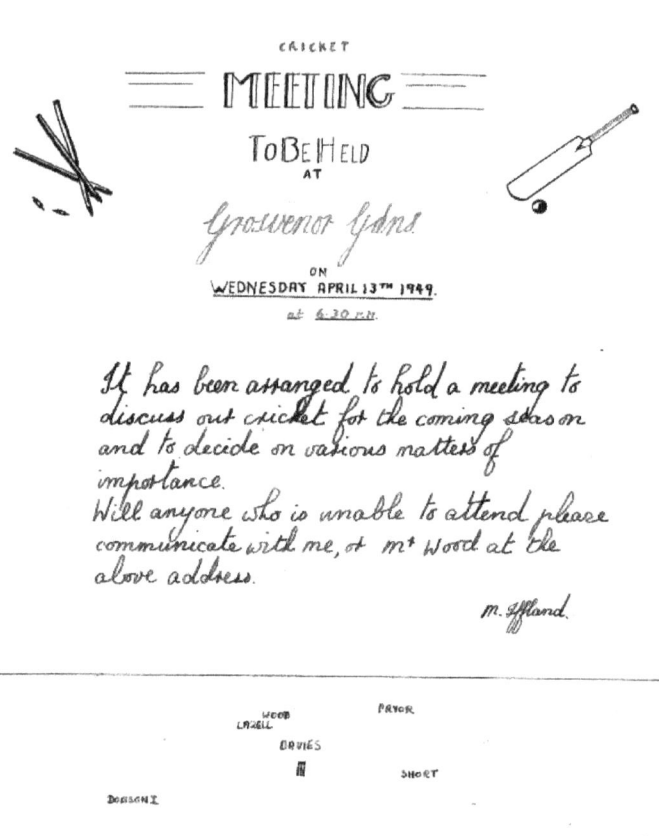

CRICKET

MEETING

ToBe Held
AT

Grosvenor Gdns

ON
WEDNESDAY APRIL 13TH 1949.
at 6.30 P.M.

It has been arranged to hold a meeting to
discuss our cricket for the coming season
and to decide on various matters of
importance.
Will anyone who is unable to attend please
communicate with me, or Mr Wood at the
above address.

M. Iffland.

WOOD
LAZELL

PRYOR

DAVIES

SHORT

DOBSON I

MEIR

CORBETT

SMALL I

IFFLAND

THACKER

Reserve Dodge

We cleared and levelled to the best of our ability a pitch in the centre of the field and invited a North Ockendon team to play us, similarly with a team from my old school. Many happy hours and days were spent in this way with parents helping with refreshments and scoring. A lovely lady whom we encouraged to score for us was Mrs Wood, who understood young boys very well and discreetly displayed her ample assets. Looking back, it really did seem that summer was eternal compared to the rush of seasons I now find as an old man.

It was about this time that Alan and I, on our Saturday morning jaunts, wearing our Harris tweed jackets or blazers, went into the centre of Upminster and first saw the girl who was to become my wife, coming out of Woolworths in Corbets Tey Road. We were both enamoured by this beautiful young girl and found out who she was and where she lived. I began to find a way to speak with her.

Me aged 18 © CA Lansley

Brenda Smith aged 16
© CA Lansley

My grandparents were very strict in their religious beliefs and tried to bring us up in the observance of good behaviour, with due respect for Sunday Christian worship. I was enrolled, along with Alan, my brother John, John Greenfield, and Peter, in the Sunday afternoon Crusaders Union Bible classes and attended at Miss Vellacott's home in Hall Lane. In addition, we were expected to attend Church or Chapel service either in the morning or the evening on a Sunday. As we grew older and the lure of other interests claimed our attention, we often skipped services and learnt other social graces, making ourselves known to the young ladies of Upminster. But looking back, the grounding I received at home gave me a sound ethical basis for my life for which I am grateful.

Perhaps, because I was unruly, I had a difficult time with my grandmother, whereas I generally got on very well with my grandfather as I learnt of his hardships in life. Often I would feel singled out or unduly restrained by my grandmother, compared to my brighter brother John and my younger brother Edgar. It appeared to me that they could do little wrong and that I made all the mistakes. Perhaps it was so, but I resented it deeply. In one altercation as she tried to hit me with the fire poker, I dodged around the dining room table to avoid her and she said:

"You are nothing. You have nothing and you never will be anything."

With the help of my dear Brenda, I proved her wrong.

9
SCHOOL LEAVER

During school holiday periods, a local Land Surveyor, Mr J.A. Story, had invited me to join with his son Robert, in assisting him on small surveys, holding the end of a tape or rod. He paid me a small amount, counted out after he had delved into his huge plus fours' pocket full of coins. It must have been uncomfortable to have all those jangling about in his pocket. No thought of credit cards then.

When in December 1948 I left school, my grandfather took me to Shoreditch, East London to try and find me employment in the cabinet making business, but everywhere we tried was the same: first you must enrol at one of the training colleges and learn the trade before we can employ you. As it had become imperative that I contribute to the household expenses, I had to find employment. Recalling my casual work for Mr Story, an interview was arranged and initially I was taken on an 'as and when' basis until the 14th of March 1949 when he took me on as a full-time Assistant.

On the 15th of March all clothing came off rationing. The effects of the war had lasted a long time but in many other respects, rationing was still in force.

John, Edgar and me © CA Lansley

Employment with Mr Story did not mean that I would be out surveying all the time. Generally, I was the 'dogsbody' doing all and sundry, digging the Story's allotment, cutting their lawn, running errands, but at least I was earning £3.10.0 a week and making a small contribution to my upkeep.

At the same time he gave me the opportunity to learn draughtsmanship, first by long practice, pages and pages of identical proportioned 'pot-hooks' as all the drawings at this time were hand lettered and 'pot-hooks' were the basis of most lettering. This reminded me of when we first came to England in 1939, that probably on Father's instructions, we had been required to fill small exercise books with identical curves and hooks to be able to write German script. (I sent

John's little copy book to his wife Thea some years ago). German script and heel clicking soon stopped.

My copy book © CA Lansley

Mr Story's encouragement and guidance meant that before long my lettering was passable, I could use the 'French' curves, use set squares and rule lines using two-bladed 'ruling pens'. He also taught me how to set up a tripod and make observations, both horizontal and vertical, with an old theodolite, understanding its vernier scale. Mr Story was an excellent teacher with patience and humour. When we were out in the field and he had a 'Woodbine' cigarette stub in his mouth, talking to passing dogs, with the theodolite over his shoulder, I felt part of the team. He reminded me that in surveying for New Towns and the like, we were doing 'work of national importance'.

Once, when in early March I was learning to use Indian ink for my line practice, to my horror, I knocked the bottle off my desk with the result of ink on the carpet! I overcame my fear of retribution and called Mr Story. There was a calm assessment of the situation and a rapid response: milk from the kitchen, blotting paper and old cloths. There was no shouting or blaming, just reassuring me as a father would. Happily, 80% came out of the carpet, but it taught me a lesson of care and compassion.

Later, Mr Story insisted on diary keeping for work details such as hours worked, expenses and eventually car running details. I had started a diary while still at school and though I do not have them all at this time, many remain and take me back to all sorts of memories, some happy but others sad. Particularly, I find it interesting to trace the history of my cars, which I hope to cover another time.

Peter McInery's parents had invited a French boy, Jean Roger Hardy, to stay with them in the summer of 1948, and we all went about together, visiting London. After Peter's death, Jean wrote and invited me to make the return trip that Peter would have made. I accepted, and in August 1950 spent an exciting holiday in their flat and was shown the sights of Paris. I recall walking along the Champs-Élysées and seeing ice creams for sale, but as each cost about ten shillings, we could not afford one. At home it would have been just six pence!

Madame Hardy cooked a delicious rabbit stew, something I had not previously enjoyed, the secret being how it had been cooked with wine, so, in the (unfulfilled) hope that Mother would cook me the same, Madame wrote the following recipe down for me on an old piece of paper which I have just unearthed from my documents!

Rabbit in 'Civet'

Take a young rabbit. Cut it into small pieces, and cook in butter or lard till the pieces are golden, then put flour (1 or 2 soup spoons).

When the flour is golden also add wine to cover the rabbit, then let it cook very slowly for two hours (add salt, pepper, thyme, parsley, onions).

When adding wine, must boil but then simmer slowly.

On leaving, Madame Hardy, who had been so kind, presented me with a watercolour she had painted of a French chateau. It hangs in our home today.

On the 2nd of September 1950 I had to register for National Service and undergo a full medical examination.

In early November 1950 I was to assist Reg Heath and Derek Browning, both of whom had recently joined Mr

Story as surveyors. We were instructed by Dowsett Engineering Construction Ltd (on whose notepaper I had written to my girlfriend when sheltering on site from a downpour. I have just found and re-read this letter, fifty-eight years later, hence my recollections!) We were to survey and set out an area for the Battersea Park Festival Gardens, London. The 'Festival of Britain', a showcase on the South Bank adjacent to Battersea Bridge, was intended to brighten the lives of people after so many years of austerity.

Different aspects of the design included the 'Skylon', a tapering finger in the sky, the 'Dome of Discovery' and 'Emmet's Railway'. Emmet was a popular cartoonist whose mad designs had to be physically set out on the ground for line and level so that the engineers could correctly erect the steel framework and rails, all in conditions of cold, rain and mud, as I recorded on the 9th of November. Another thing I also noted was that when it rained, all the site staff downed tools, even those working indoors! Union Rules!

By this time I was trying to fight off the competition for the affection of the 'girl coming out of Woolworth's', Brenda Smith, and while in Paris had bought her a small silver 'Fleur de Lyse' brooch which she still has. Soon after my return on the 23rd of November, I received my National Service Call-Up papers which were to change my life dramatically.

10
NATIONAL SERVICE IN THE ROYAL REGIMENT OF ARTILLERY

My joining papers © CA Lansley

Earlier in 1950, the period one was expected to serve was eighteen months. However this was increased to two years just as our intake had to report. To compensate for this extra time to be served, for the last six months we were all to be paid on the same basis as a regular soldier, not that this amounted to very much. I do not recall suddenly feeling that much better off!

Nothing in my previous life had prepared me for the embarrassment of an Army pre-entry medical examination, which for some reason I had vaguely expected to fail, but was delighted to pass as A1 fit. In due course I received reporting instructions and a travel warrant.

My happy friendship with Brenda Smith had continued and the evening prior to departure we went for the 'Last Supper', or so it felt, at the Green Lantern Restaurant in Hornchurch.

The next day, the 7th of December 1950, with considerable trepidation, I sct out to join the group of young men heading for the Royal Artillery Barracks at Oswestry, Salop. On eventual arrival with the many others, who like myself had heard of the short haircut rule, I noted that all had visited the barber.

I am at the right end of the back row. © *CA Lansley*

We were herded together and issued our military numbers, mine being 22438959, with threats of all manner of evil things that would befall us if we could not repeat it without hesitation when challenged. We were then 'fallen-in' and marched to the Quartermaster's store where we were loaded with uniforms, greatcoats, webbing belts, pouches, gaiters, a rifle, etc. and worse, coarse 'long-johns,' and then off to our quarters. These consisted of long Nissan huts, each with circular iron stoves in the centre and at the end of the room, the exposed chimneys going out through the roof. A dozen or so beds were lined up on each side (I cannot recall exactly how many). We had been marched there by our Lance Bombadier (known in other army groups as Corporal), who would ensure that we learnt to lay out all our kit, towels folded just so, everything presented in one format. For the slightest deviation, one would earn a bellow or be given extra duties to perform. The Lance Bombardier's quarters was a small separate room opposite the 'ablutions.' Regardless of our already short hair, we were forced to visit the site barber, not only reducing our hair further but also our meagre pocket money.

On the 10th we were given sight and intelligence tests which we all appeared to pass, followed by a lecture on military discipline and a further medical examination with the admonition, 'If you look for it, you will find it. If you find it, you will get it. If you get it, you have had it!'

Our basic ten-week' 'square bashing' began on a cold winter's day, the 13th of December 1950, after it had snowed. The normal routine of 'spit and polishing,' bullying and parades followed which I am glad to put out of my mind. However, all the recruits were in the same boat and we coped.

On completion of basic training and subsequent interviews, I had identified my interest in surveying and was posted to Salisbury Plain, Gibraltar Battery, 192 Independent Survey Training Battery R.A. Larkhill, Wiltshire and on arrival was put into Squad 116. Our training was designed to provide the gunners with coordinated information enabling them to accurately locate enemy gun positions.

Basic survey training was intended to provide competence in theodolite observations, minor instrument adjustments, map reading, trigonometry and measurement, all in the context of military exercise. We were then allocated to different survey groups. Artillery Survey comprised of Radar Troop, Sound Ranging, Flash Spotting and Survey Troop, all with the same aim, to provide our gunners with coordinate positions of the enemy, each by its own speciality.

Radar Troop had large vehicles containing radar equipment which sat dangerously on the top of hills and whose readings would provide a location of the enemy guns as they fired. Sound Ranging would attempt the same, but less conspicuously, by having a string of linked microphones set out, once again to intersect and pinpoint the noise of the enemy guns. Flash Spotters had the most dangerous job during wartime in that they perched on high vantage points to actually observe the enemy guns' flash and take simple theodolite readings from pre-coordinated positions in such places as church towers and radio transmit the data to base. In action, their life expectancy was not very long. I was posted to Survey Troop. Our prime objective was to link our various positions by establishing a coordinate framework system on the ground whereby the various methods of locating could be linked to local or battlefield topographical map grids.

When we were on exercises undertaking triangulation schemes, battle plans or learning to drive Jeeps and Land Rovers, I was reasonably happy. Several of us had applied for Provisional Driving Licenses but on my first excursion I found it quite alarming to have to drive through the centre of Salisbury in a Land Rover. However, the vehicle and I survived my first lesson.

Unfortunately, during the first winter when learning to drive, I was taken by my instructor through icy winding Wiltshire lanes along which I was making good progress until at a sharp bend he suddenly ordered 'brake', which I did, a little too sharply, and the Land Rover continued straight on and straddled the hedge on the far side. Here was no way that we could recover it manually, although we tried. As a result, I was put on a Charge but at the hearing before the Battery Commander the instructor was held to blame.

On the 8th of April 1951, one of our instructor officers, Lt. Lewis, offered to put me up for a commission, but from what I had already learnt of Army life there was no desire in me to sign on for a further three years, assuming that I would have passed the W.O.S.B. (War Office Selection Board).

On the 27th of April, we received our results and I had passed the Survey Trade Test. I was then allowed to sew on to my tunic sleeve the 'S' to signify this success.

On the 2nd of July, my birthday, I passed my Driving Test, once again being taken through the busy Salisbury streets.

I am centre back row © CA Lansley

Subsequently, there was a second motoring incident after I had passed my driving test. Land Rovers were allocated to drivers and the driver was responsible not only for cleanliness but also that maintenance was carried out. The nearside door of my vehicle had a faulty catch, and try as I could to get the M.T. workshops to repair it, it still would fly open when leaned against. I therefore wrote out a large 'Caution' notice and fixed it to the dashboard. On this occasion I was asked to drive Captain Hearn, one of our officers, on an exercise, and just as we were negotiating a bend, he leant on the door which flew open and he fell out. Fortunately he was not seriously hurt, but of course seat belts were not fitted at this time. Once again I was on a Charge. Capt. Hearn bore me no ill will and his testimony helped me at the hearing.

My nineteenth birthday, on the 2ⁿᵈ of July 1951, on leave, on Woolacombe beach with Brenda. © CA Lansley

Life became tedious. We were being used just as 'dogsbodies' for such tasks as erecting tents for Territorial soldiers who came out to train on Salisbury Plain. A small group of us had heard that there were courses for which one could apply and we decided that any course would be better than this boredom. We learnt of an interesting Draughtsman's course which was available at the Royal Engineers' School of Military Survey, Hermitage, Newbury and applied. Three of us were successful and it proved interesting and challenging in a schoolboy way, in that once having mastered the art of sketching and using ruling pen and compass, which I had begun with Mr Story, the draughtsman's task was to get as close as possible to enemy lines and sketch the layout of buildings, trees, road junctions and bridges, to prepare for our forces as they advanced. While it was exciting as an exercise, in wartime it would have been rather hazardous. We were posted to Two Troop-B Squadron, School of Military Survey R.E. Hermitage, Newbury.

Our time at Newbury passed well, with the exception of one occasion, when at the beginning of August, returning to camp from Paddington on a Sunday night, we found that the first train direct to Newbury was the next Wednesday morning! Panic! Eventually, we managed to catch a train to Reading. I then hitch-hiked on the back of a friendly motorcyclist for twenty-five minutes; then walked to Thatcham (three miles from Newbury), where another car gave me a lift into Newbury. I had to walk the last four miles to the camp, arriving about 02.20 hrs, unfortunately wearing a brand-new pair of shoes. On arrival at camp my feet were bleeding. Not easily forgotten. Walking at night, many cars passed but would not stop. At this time motorists would usually stop to give a lift to men in uniform, but not those in 'civvies.'

We attended all the lectures, which were interesting, and followed up with field exercises to put our training into practice. We had to take our turn to Mount Guard at Hermitage, but our Guards here meant we had to have fixed bayonets on our rifles, which had never been the case on our Artillery Guard duties. All too soon our course was finished and we had to report back to Larkhill.

The time passed slowly with the odd battle plan or survey exercise, as when we moved to an Artillery Barracks near the cliffs at Bude, Barnstable, Devon. It was there that we learnt on the 6th of February 1952 the sad news that King George V1 had died and flags were flown at half-mast. Our troop was to be firing on the ranges, but before we began, all men faced the targets and observed two minutes' silence.

On the 1st of March 1952, twenty men from our regiment were posted to Korea, not to be envied as I believe a number of National Servicemen lost their lives. Back at Larkhill, on the 27th of March, we moved from our old barrack blocks to brick-built quarters at Roberts Lines, and it was snowing, as were the following days. John Cave, a fellow Surveyor gunner, owned a car and drove a group of us to London as he had on several occasions and we all contributed to the costs. This time, on the 31st of March, as we returned after the weekend, we slid into a snowdrift but were dug out by some friendly policemen. Fortunately, we managed to get back to barracks in time for morning lectures. In addition to training for survey, arms drill, and very frequent barrack room inspections, different sections had to form the Camp Guard. The half a dozen ordered to 'Mount Guard' were always in their best kit, all spit and polish, and the Guard Commander would critically inspect the formed-up men for the slightest speck or other blemish. He selected one man from the motley guard crew who was 'best on parade' for his turnout. Such a person was called the 'Stickman', a cherished position but I cannot recall why! I am sure some benefit accrued to him. Occasionally, I received this 'distinction'.

The 29th of May was Regimental Sports Day. There was fierce competition between the units and I was press-ganged into performing. Athletics had never been my forte but I managed to scrape fifth in the 440m, third in the 880m, but won the high jump at 5ft 4 inches (the same as when I was a schoolboy in 1948, no improvement!)

On the 26th of July 1952, I received, on Battery Orders, promotion to the dizzy heights of Lance Bombadier. This, together with the 'S' sewn on my sleeve for having passed the Survey Trade Test, made me feel an individual, standing out from the crowd. Shooting on the ranges with a .303 rifle, I could only reach 2nd Class shot, but performed better with the Sten gun which was more by luck as it can be a very erratic weapon, often fired from the hip.

Eventually, there came the excitement of 'demob' and the anticipation of no longer being separated from my family and friends, especially from Brenda Smith. I had become very fond of her and saw her whenever I was home on leave.

In December 1952, I received my Discharge Papers, had a final Medical and was instructed to report for ongoing Territorial Army service. It was a requirement that National Servicemen should continue their commitment to the Services by regular part-time training and exercises. I was to report to the Honourable Artillery Company's headquarters in London and hand in my kit from when I would be free to continue with my civilian life. However, I had to make myself available for weekend camps, usually at Bisley for rifle shooting practice. It was very different from regular service life, friendly, and almost like a club.

I restarted working for Mr Story on the 15th of December 1952. However, I was ordered to report for an interview with the HAC Battery Commander on the evening of the 30th of December. I cannot recall what was discussed, but probably my part-time responsibilities.

In January 1953, storms raged first across the northwest of the UK and then split, coming across and down the east coast where largely unprepared coastal towns and villages were devastated by unprecedented high tides and exceptional winds resulting in a large loss of life. Nearby Canvey Island was low lying and had its seawalls breached in many places with people trying to survive, clinging to the roofs of their chalet homes. Unhappily, all too many young and elderly people died of exposure or drowning.

Mr Story had an urgent request for surveying assistance to check the heights of the remaining sections of the seawall around Canvey Island and produce data for cross sections through the walls to enable a rapid repair response and uplift. I had only just left the Army, wherein Artillery survey theodolite work was normal, but spirit levelling and reading the graduated staff was unknown. I was given a day and a half crash course at the old miniature golf course, 'our cricket ground,' by a new Story surveyor, Reg Heath and then I was sent down to join the various bodies and organisations who were trying to make sense of the disaster.

For 'chainman', I had an old lorry driver who ferried me around in his huge noisy diesel lorry, going from one remaining section of sea wall to another, where possible, but the majority was on foot. Levelling is not a complex operation, but the reliability of the results is essential. The method of booking and cross-checking gives certainty of results, in that measurements start from an Ordnance Survey or other known height datum (benchmark) and are taken in a looping circuit ending on the same point or another of known height. Simple arithmetic proved the 'closure' or identified when the tolerance had not been met. Apart from the slowness due to my inexperience, this first test of working on my own passed off well.

This was then followed in the subsequent months by working on land surveys for post-war New Towns such as Peterlee, Newton Aycliffe and many others. I acted as Assistant to a stocky ex-Army Sergeant, John M. Webb, who had been at the wartime Dunkirk evacuation and had known Mr Story during this time and subsequently joined him, while I was doing my National Service.

11
MY FIRST TRIP TO THE MIDDLE EAST

In April 1953 John Webb and I were asked to undertake a topographical survey for London Consulting Engineers, Maunsell, Posford and Pavry of a site at Eski Mosul, north of Mosul, Iraq, for a proposed huge dam across the River Tigris. The party included geologists and drillers with their rigs, testing the ground conditions which were mainly made of gypsum.

Aerial view of the proposed dam site © Google Earth

We flew out from Heathrow on a BOAC 'Argonaut' via Frankfurt, Rome, Istanbul, Mafraq (Jordan) and on to Baghdad. On board was the young Prince Faisal, who shortly was to become King of Iraq and was met with all due ceremony at the airport.

The first difficulty we experienced was clearing our equipment through Customs. All the normal procedures had to be completed. Maunsell's Iraqi driver, Fuad, met us and took us through the mad Baghdad traffic to the Sinbad Hotel, very close to our client's Office in Rashid Street.

Sinbad Hotel card © CA Lansley

We needed passport-type photos for temporary Resident's Visas and Police clearance.

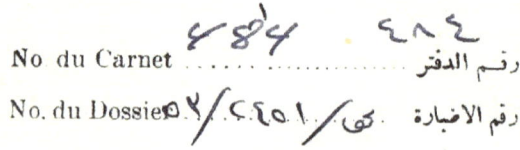

No du Carnet .... رقم الدفتر

No. du Dossier .... رقم الاضبارة

Signature du titulaire on   توقيع حامله او بصمة

son empreinte digitale.   ابهامه الايسر

Temporary Resident's Visa © CA Lansley

While walking down Rashid Street, I was accosted by a young man who whispered, "Nice girl for 'exhibish'?" I was somewhat taken aback, but soon realised that these touts were all over Baghdad. I was not tempted! The few days in town were very pleasant compared to the tough life we would lead under canvas once we arrived at Eski Mosul.

We had been made temporary members of the Alwiyah Club,[10] with its swimming pool and very pleasant social life, especially on a Friday, which, of course, is the Muslim rest day.

While we were still in Baghdad, the celebrations for the new King Faisal's Coronation started, with military parades through the town which we watched from the office balcony.

King Faisal's Coronation Procession © CA Lansley

Before the equipment and provisions could be taken to the site, a new section of road had to be cut through the rough terrain between Mosul and the survey site north, at Eski Mosul, to enable the trucks carrying all the gear to pass. This

---

[10] The Alwiyah Club was one of the best elite social clubs of Baghdad. It is one of Baghdad's oldest institutions and was established in 1924. The Alwiyah Club continues to stand as a testament to Baghdad's rich cultural and social heritage, and the Iraq Britain Business Council (IBBC) hosted a distinguished Reception and Dinner at this iconic venue on the 8th of January 2025.

was done using a bulldozer-bladed grader. All this took some time during which I was asked to take survey-level readings for a new section of road leading to the proposed Daura Oil Refinery. We were getting up before dawn, driving to the site in a taxi with my Arab assistants and working until the heat made it impossible to obtain accurate readings, generally beyond about ten a.m. Eventually, all was ready. John Webb had already gone on ahead and I caught the overnight train, which sensibly travelled almost at walking pace so one could sleep and arrive at Mosul station in time for breakfast. My lasting impression of this place was of arriving and having breakfast at the station buffet which had 'camel thorn' screens at the windows down which trickled water, as a form of air conditioning, while a sandstorm raged outside, covering everything in fine sand. Also, I had never before seen such huge piles of watermelons as I saw in the station yard.

I was collected by one of the camp drivers and we bounced our way northwards through the recently completed dirt track to the east bank of the Tigris which was to be our base. Tents had been erected, and I had the luxury of a shower, comprising a kerosene tin with holes punched in the bottom raised on a frame and fed by a hose, pumped from a borehole, all modern living!

Our surveying task began immediately with a reconnoitre of the site, and an apportionment of Webb's and my area to be surveyed. Local men had been employed to act as survey assistants and also as armed guards, although we experienced no problems that I can recall. Far from it, we were made welcome as providers of employment and were even invited to join in the celebrations for a local wedding.

My survey team © *CA Lansley*

We witnessed the ceremony of proving that the bride had been a virgin, by her brothers coming out of the nuptial tent waving a bloodied sheet, whereupon the men all danced around firing their rifles in the air in celebration. I believe that sometimes this is faked, but that is not so likely in the countryside. Unhappily, this traditional ceremony brought death to over forty men, women and children in May 2004 when the occupying American forces took this to be the

Iraqis trying to shoot at them and with their helicopter gunships demolished the place.[11]

Me © CA Lansley

My twenty-first birthday on the 2nd of July was seemingly ignored; no congratulations, cards or letters from home. Only when the day's work had been done did I receive my mail and the congratulations of the site team, with watermelon and a beer. Amongst the cards was a letter from

---

[11] This is the Mukaradeeb wedding party massacre which refers to the U.S. military's attack on a wedding party in Mukaradeeb, a small village in Anbar Province, Iraq near the border with Syria, on 19 May 2004. The attack killed 42 civilians and wounded many others. The U.S. military denied that a wedding had been hit, claiming the location was a legitimate military target and that insurgents had been killed. U.S. military generals refused to apologize for the massacre. See https://en.wikipedia.org/wiki/Mukaradeeb_wedding_party_massacre#Incident

my father in Germany,[12] in reply to one I had written earlier in June, my first letter to him as an adult.

---

[12] This is a transcription of the undated letter, sent around the time of my father's 21st birthday, the 2nd of July 1953:
"We are all sinners.
My dear boy, I should so very much like to hear more of you, of Hans and Edgar and also of your mother, of your grandparents and Margaret. I am glad you found a dear friend and I wish you both God's blessing. Please write about your life in Iraq. I am interested in everything. And I do hope to see you perhaps with your [....y] some day here in Germany.
Enclosed some photos.
Could you send me [some] of yours and of all the others? Your loving father,
Hans
And one more thing, my boy.
I congratulate most heartily on your 21st birthday. Many happy returns of the day and God's blessing.
Some of your hair, when you had fallen in a lime pit in Salonika."

I was excited and confused, raising in me all the questions since we parted at Hanau Station in July 1939. The letter enclosed a little packet, in which was a lock of my bleached blonde hair that he had kept from the time when, in Salonika, I fell into a lime pit. One of the BOAC stop-offs on the way home was to be Frankfurt, so I resolved to see my father and try to get some answers. When I wrote, I did not know my final departure date from Iraq. Certainly, I had not thought of the consequences back home, where, when they learnt of my visit, I was labelled a traitor.

The topographic survey continued well. Odd memories come back of Jock, one of the Wimpey drillers at camp, inviting me one evening to join him on a visit to Mosul. In fact, he took me to a place on the outskirts where, within a large walled 'township', lived outcasts with police guarding the gates, thronged with men looking for prostitutes. This was a 'Kalachia' (if spelt correctly), where women who had been thrown out by their families for becoming pregnant out of wedlock, lived communally, often after first being mutilated. We saw women whose noses had been cut off by their families, absolutely barbaric, and frightening. These women never left their small village, and a thriving market catered for them and their visitors. As our Jeep drove through the township, women were calling out to us from their huts. I truly thought I was in Sodom and Gomorrah and asked Jock to take me home. It was a sad reflection on men, treating women that way.

A happier recollection was about halfway through our time at Eski Mosul. We had a day off with a trip north to visit the mountains of Kurdish Iraq. On rough roads and tracks, we headed north and found the small town of Sheikh Adi where fig trees grew out of the rocky scree of the mountainside and peace and shade were found in the shelter of the stone houses. It made such a great impression on me, that in later years, I thought this would be an ideal place to spend one's last days. Unhappily, with the terrible developments in these past years, with our invasion of Iraq, the peacefulness will have gone as fighting and insurgency continue with daily deaths, even in these remote areas.

Continuing with the survey for the dam site, we swam daily in the Tigris which flowed past our camp, while avoiding the odd donkey carcass floating downstream. The Wimpey drillers had provided all life's facilities: a deep borehole over which stood a chair with no seat. As it became much hotter, a mud brick hut was built for us by locals, as an office cum rest room. We even had a badminton net fixed up for our 'civilised' living.

John Webb (L) and Jock the Wimpey driller © CA Lansley

On one occasion, John Webb wagered me a tin of 50 cigarettes that I could not swim across the swiftly flowing Tigris to the west bank. I took up the challenge and eventually made it across, ending up several hundred yards downstream, then having to make the return crossing, by which time I was exhausted. I have never forgotten that Webb welched on his bet and never gave me the cigarettes; perhaps for my health it was a good thing!

Thinking again about my father's letter, while at camp, I had decided to try and contact my father in Germany and subsequently wrote to him at the beginning of June 1953. I have no recollection of how I obtained his address; perhaps I simply put Herr Lehrer Johannes Iffland, Michelstadt. However, he did receive it and replied to me on the 11th of June.

On completion of the topographic survey, we returned to Baghdad. From Baghdad, I was asked to undertake a survey for a proposed new bridge at Samawa, which Maunsell Engineer John Swansbourne was to design. After our retirements, John Swansbourne and I continued our friendship over very many years, ending only when Brenda and I attended his funeral on the 25th of February 2009.

The Stone Lion at Babylon © Claire Lansley

Before this, he and I visited the site of Babylon, with its Stone Lion: all this was, of course, before Saddam Hussein defaced the ancient structures there. I stayed at a rest house at Hilla, south of Baghdad. It was the time of Ashoora when Shia Arabs remember the martyrdom of their Saint Hussain. To symbolically atone for having deserted him, the Shias process through the towns and villages, flagellating themselves with swords and chains, working up into a frenzy with blood running down their heads and bodies.

Ashoora[13] *© CA Lansley*

Ashoora © CA Lansley

---

[13] Sketch by Martyn Iffland

I was ordered to remain in the rest house at all times that they were parading, which was mainly late afternoon which enabled me in the early morning to mark out my traverse and make my observations (a quadrilateral spanning the river, all of whose angles had to be observed and the bases on each bank measured to enable me to calculate the crossing distance.) Nowadays, with electronic surveying measuring equipment, the task would be completed very rapidly. It was an interesting small survey conducted amid the pomegranate trees along the banks. While I was taking my readings, a shot rang out, and later I heard that a prisoner on the far bank had escaped and had been shot.

I came back to Maunsell's office in Baghdad, where John Swansbourne was the Design Engineer for the bridge and as soon as I had proved all my calculations, I was invited to a cricket weekend held annually at Kirkuk. It was a hot and dusty journey by car but I was welcomed with iced coffee and the offer of a cool shower. I lodged with one of the oil company's married staff and thoroughly enjoyed the short relaxation after the hard work regime. On returning to Baghdad, I handed over all the data and began a nervous journey home via Frankfurt.

12
REUNION WITH FATHER AND RETURN TO IRAQ

After we had left our first refuelling stop at Mafraq, Jordan, I was scanning the land and sea and from the brochure maps provided, I realised that our route passed over Salonika, which excited me and as I was looking out, I was able to distinctly make out the shape of the White Tower on the seafront at Salonika.

The White Tower at Salonika © CA Lansley

I recall well my unannounced arrival at Frankfurt airport, as I did not know until the last moment when I would get a flight. It was all quite an adventure but I had no ability to speak German after fourteen years of only speaking English. Eventually, I got myself to the main railway station and found my way onto a train. We passed through Hanau, and I became so excited that I tried to explain to a young fellow traveller that this was my birthplace and even showed him my passport. The journey continued on the hard wooden train bench seats, which were then the norm. Somehow, I expected the train to stop at Michelstadt but it sailed through to Erbach. My father was, however, living in Erbach.

On the journey, I met a young man named Gunter Fornhoff. He was going to visit his girlfriend who lived in a street immediately adjoining 12 Johann Erhardt Strasse, where Father lived, and as it was getting late said we should first go to her home and then they would check if my father was at home. His girlfriend's mother gave me some refreshments while they checked. It was Sunday, and my father was away for the weekend.

I wanted to find a small hotel, but they insisted that I stay the night with them and made me up a bed on their living room floor. I shall never forget their kindness. I had come from the heat of Iraq to a chilly evening in Germany, and sleeping with the window wide open, I woke with a cold. Next morning, they found out that my father was back and Gunter took me round, leaving me at the entrance. I went up and knocked and the door was opened by a thin-faced woman I had never seen before, dressed mainly in black. It was Hedwig who had replaced my mother, and while she was friendly, I was instinctively aloof.

The small modern flat had a central corridor leading to the living room at the far end on the right and I was escorted down. The room was filled on the left wall with books, and Father was sitting, waiting. It must have been as difficult for him as it was for me. I could not speak to him in German and his English was very hesitant for which he apologised.

It was very formal and we shook hands. It is hazy how long we talked or even the topics; both of us were uncomfortable. I did, though, stress the grief and disappointment that he had deserted Mother. He tried to explain that Germany thought they would win the war and that we would never meet again. After my protestations, he said that he was now an older and wiser man and that he regretted his actions. He said that as he had been a reasonably young man without a wife for all those years and thinking he would never see his family again, I should try to understand that he had succumbed to a new relationship.

Father needed to go to the bank and it is my first real recollection of their seven-year-old daughter Ursula. The three of us together walked the short distance, but it started to rain and I put my jacket around her shoulders. Again, my memory fails me as to whether I remained another day, but I recall my Uncle Franz taking Father and me by car to the airport and that Father bought me a small packet of pretzels. I have always enjoyed pretzels.

As can be imagined, on my return I did not receive much of a welcome from my family in Upminster.

Once back in England, I briefly continued surveying sites in England, but on the 22nd of January 1954, I was again a member of the team flown out to Iraq to survey the route of a proposed railway from Baghdad to Basra. We were to start the section from Nasiriyah to Kut. As was always the case, clearing our surveying equipment of theodolites, levels and ancillary gear through Customs, and registering with authorities took time, but with the help of Fuad, the friendly company driver and handyman, we were eventually successful and hired vehicles to make our way to Nasiriyah. There, we had the luxury of a two-storey mud brick house as it was cold and wet. From my diary, I noted that at this time, I was paid three-weekly, for which I earned, including an overseas allowance, £25.3.0. The weather was unpleasant, and our Land Rover was getting stuck in the mud.

The proposed line was walked, and local men were employed as chainmen and armed guards. All these people were provided, for a charge, by the local Sheikh, but as we progressed down the line, new negotiations had to be made with each Sheikh as we entered their territory. We then moved down to Shatra on the 8th of February, managing to get another house, but this time in a noisy populated area.

Shatra[14] © *CA Lansley*

A fellow surveyor, Eric Anderson and I decided to visit the nearby Biblical site of 'Ur of the Chaldees' on Friday the 26th of February 1954. The site contains a huge structure, the 'Ziggurat,' which was a Temple to the Sun God. Complex mathematical tables had been discovered there, which demonstrated the corrections that the architects needed to apply so that the walls were built outward-curving but giving the appearance of being flat-sided. This was quite incredible at this time in history. Wonderful treasures had been discovered there in the burial pits by Sir Leonard Woolley and others, among them the Harp and the Golden Seal, which had been made soon after the Biblical Flood.

---

[14] I am first left in the back row in the far right-hand corner.

The Ziggurat at Ur © CA Lansley

Ur was the Prophet Abraham's birthplace. We found the place where the burial pits had been excavated. At a considerable depth, at the side of one of the diggings, I found the exposed side of a small pot protruding. Eric (Andy) Anderson clambered slowly down and very carefully released it. We became very excited on seeing that the ancient potter had left his finger marks on the side. I recovered a second pot, some 'cuneiform' writing, sections of a human skull and a small hollow item.

© CA Lansley

© CA Lansley

The photograph gives an idea of the great depth of the excavations © CA Lansley

Back at camp, the survey continued in spite of the thunderstorms and heavy rain. We moved further down to Khalat Sukir on the 14th of March. It was windy and visibility was poor, when on the 23rd of March our camp was flooded and then yet again on the 3rd of April, when some of our drawings were damaged. Heavy rain on the 6th made roads impossible to pass. We continued as best as we could along the proposed line, when on the 10th of April, moving camp once more, our lorry got bogged down. Finally, it managed to be towed clear and we moved on to Kut al Hai. By this time, a major part of Southern Iraq was flooded. We had endured some pretty rough conditions, but then in the space of a week, we were royally entertained by two local Sheikhs.

On the 23rd of April, Sheikh Balasim Jasime invited us all to dinner in the evening. His palace was surrounded by a large courtyard with high walls, outside of which lived the poor whose labours sustained such opulence. The invitations came as quite a surprise. All the local officials were there, as well as a flood relief doctor from Egypt who had studied at Moorfields Eye Hospital, London.

The Sheikh's palace was sumptuously laid out with large, beautiful Persian carpets and suspended above, large crystal chandeliers. We all sat on colourful cushions on the floor, opposite each other, while male servants offered us all manner of delicacies imaginable. Laid out were whole sheep, pigs, etc. and huge bowls of salads, rice, khobus and chapatis. I am sure that one of our number was offered a sheep's eye! We drank wine and VAT 69 whisky.

The next day, we experienced more extensive flooding and our lorry had to take a major detour to reach us.

On Monday the 26th of April, we had our second invitation to dinner. This time, it was from Sheikh Abeyed Abdullah. My notes recall that it was rather a boring evening but very good food and mainly talking with Egyptian doctors from Cairo, all from the same Flood Relief Organisation.

After these meals, unfortunately, two of our party were ill for some days and needed a doctor's attention, but not me!

Our move to the final camp for this season was made on the 6th of May to Kut. On Tuesday the 11th it was our turn to offer hospitality and His Excellency the Mutsariph of Kut, the Chief of Police, and the Head of the Medical Department came for drinks in the evening. Unexpectedly, we received yet another invitation; this time for lunch on the 14th from the Chief Medical Officer. I have no recollection of the meal, so perhaps I did not go.

By now, the weather had become very hot, and an alleged Communist demonstration in Hai and Kut on the 21st resulted in three people being killed, but fortunately, it did not directly affect our people. Because of the flooding, roads back to Baghdad were impassable, and as I was due to report back to Baghdad, the current fieldwork having been completed, the only way was to fly back in a small Auster aircraft. I was airsick! Back in Baghdad, I completed my calculations and plotting before collecting the exit visa. A letter from Mr Story on Whit Monday 1954 told me of a pay rise; naturally, I was pleased!

13
RETURN FROM IRAQ AND A PROPOSAL

I started the journey home on the 10th of June 1954, stopping off in Frankfurt where I was met by my Uncle Franz. The next day, for the first time in fifteen years, I saw my Godfather, Onkel Wilhelm Jung, who was lying seriously ill in bed.

Onkel Franz had collected me from the airport and the next day took me to the cemetery in Erbach, where Father had been buried only such a short time before,[15] and left me to contemplate what might have been. I had written to Father from Iraq, saying that I would like to meet him once more and that I intended to marry Brenda. He had offered to take me to the family diamond business in Frankfurt, where I could buy a 'stone of the first water' and have it set.

Onkel Franz took me to the family jewellers in Frankfurt, where we were escorted through several locked doors and guided in the selection of a diamond within my price range. Then back to Hanau, where I met Rudi again for the first time since the war. A local jeweller formed the stone into an engagement solitaire ring for Brenda as the following day, I

---

[15] Father died of pneumonia on 12th April 1954.

had to catch my onward flight to the UK. I left Frankfurt Airport on the 13ᵗʰ of June, where I was unexpectedly seen off by not only Onkel Franz but also Tante Sophie (I never saw her again after this as she died before my next visit), Tante Luise and Rosemary.

Onkel Franz, Tante Sophie, Rosemary, Tante Luise, Hetwig, me and Ursula © CA Lansley

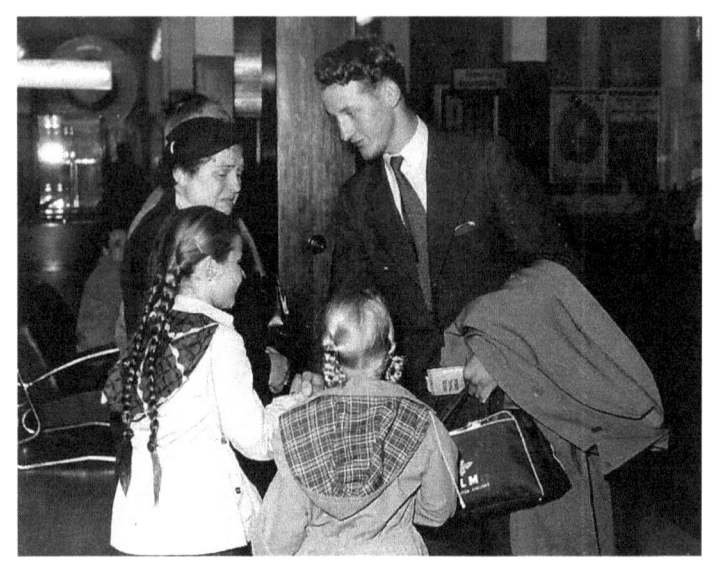

At the airport © CA Lansley

Departing Frankfurt for London © CA Lansley

I arrived at Heathrow at 11.15 p.m. to be met by Brenda, her father, and Edgar. Brenda and I sat in the back of the car, I proposed and gave her the ring, and she accepted. A happy ending to an arduous tour.

At this time, I had been told by my employer, Mr Story, that I must have my own transport, and so I spent many fruitless days looking at old wrecks. However, John Greenfield told me of a two-seater sports car he had seen in Mile End, London, a powder blue two-seater MG J2 model, JF5278. Edgar and I went up to London to see it and immediately fell in love with, and paid for it. (But with hindsight, I wish I had not. During the year that I owned it, everything that could go wrong seemed to do so.)

After many delays, I collected it on the 2nd of July 1954, having paid £131-10-00 and 13 shillings and four pence for 3 gallons of petrol. The subsequent repair costs for the following year far outweighed the initial investment.

My first car © CA Lansley

Soon after I had my MG, John Greenfield bought his wonderful machine, a 1934 Lagonda Rapier De Clifford Special CGH 602. This car was one of the few Specials built after the original car raced at Le Mans. At the time of writing, John's car is still running, though unfortunately no longer in his possession.

To add to the variety of motors between the friends, Alan first bought an air-cooled Morgan three-wheeler, but like my MG, it was unreliable, so he quickly changed to two wheels to speed him north when he was completing his National Service in the RAF. The first of his motorbikes was a Francis Barnet (water-cooled) 197cc. This was followed by a very reliable Velocette 350cc.

On the 29th of June, Mr Story gave me the task of surveying 1000 acres of Parndon, Harlow, Essex, for the proposed Harlow New Town, quite some undertaking. My assistant and I stayed at an on-site pub 'The Three Horseshoes', run by Mrs 'Aggie' Randall, a real old Essex publican who swore by washing her hair each week in beer! Some weekends, John Greenfield, Alan with his girlfriend Dylys, Brenda and other friends would come and join me after work at Parndon and get to know my landlady.

One day, we were sketching, chaining and offset measuring in a Parndon lane, when out of the hedge appeared Mr Story, who unknown to us had been watching our progress. He congratulated me and gave me an immediate pay rise!

Frequently after a weekend at home, on returning, the car would break down just as I was about to go up a hill somewhere in Essex, with nowhere to find a garage. Aggiss' Garage, Upminster, made a fortune out of me, including 'repairing' a cracked cylinder block.

That August, Brenda and I drove down to Cliftonville and I recall often being embarrassed by the awful screeching of the M.G.'s brakes. We made it safely there but got caught in a rainstorm on our return. Fortunately, we had a folding roof and new side screens that I had just bought, so we were reasonably weatherproof.

Brenda and the MG © CA Lansley

I recently made enquiries about whether the MG Owners Club had any record of my old car. The initial enquiry proved negative, but then I was delighted to receive an e-mail from a club member, with photographs of JF5278, completely re-built as original, but now painted red, and with a booster which enables her to travel at 100mph. I do not think that I ever could drive her at more than 60mph!

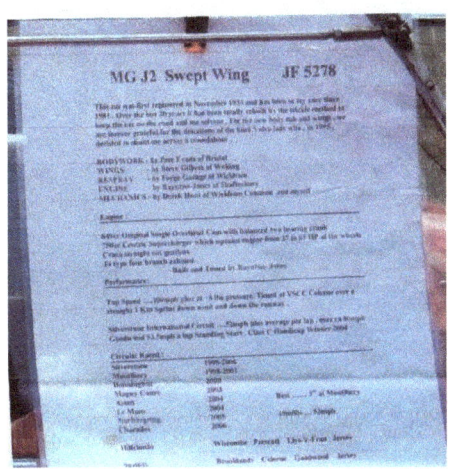

MG JF5278 © CA Lansley

In September 1954, I was called by the Honourable Artillery Company to attend a week's Territorial Army training, 'Exercise London Pride'. As I was so often overseas, I had been excused from many of the regular attendances, but in fact, after normal National Service, this was more like a week's fun. I attended training again in

November, but only a weekend shooting at Bisley, and I believe this was the last time.

14
WEDDINGS

Much of the remainder of 1954 was spent surveying for the Harlow New Town, but an important event on the 9th of July 1955 was my brother John's marriage to Thea Crowl at the Church of St. Budeaux in Plymouth. I was still occupied with the Parndon survey, but on the afternoon of the 8th of July, John, Edgar and I met Brenda at Fenchurch Street Station in my latest addition: a black Austin 8hp 1939 two door saloon JX8021, which I had bought in May from F.G. Smith (Motors) Goodmayes for £460.00. I had sold the MG, it being utterly unreliable, and I could not afford to continue spending money on it. We drove through the night, arriving at our guesthouse in the early hours with only one unnecessary stop due to a petrol blockage. I could not sleep as I had taken 'Dexedrine.'[16]

We got up at 5.30 a.m., cleaned the car, generally prepared and took John's shoes to be heeled as he was anxious about displaying them as he kneeled at the altar. We arrived at the church three-quarters of an hour early. John was uncharacteristically very nervous. The unfamiliar Roman Catholic service went well, and I was proud that John

---

[16] Dexedrine is a stimulant. My father no doubt took it to help him stay awake after working long hours and driving through the night!

had asked me to be his Best Man. We went to Mr and Mrs Crowl's home at Dovedale Road for the reception.

John and Thea Iffland © CA Lansley

John and Thea's Wedding
From left: Edgar, Auntie Dadit, Me, Brenda, John, Thea,
Bridesmaid, Theodore Crowl, Aileen Crowl © CA Lansley

The next day, Brenda, Edgar and I drove home via Paignton, Lyme Regis and Charmouth, where we stopped to bathe. Then I went back to Harlow, and Edgar flew to Germany for a two-month holiday in Michelstadt.

From now on, it was 'all systems go' preparing for our own wedding, which we had decided would be on the 17th of September at the Congregational Church, Upminster. On the 16th of August, Brenda's father Edmund, my friends Alan, John Ryley and I met at the outfitters 'Da Costa' at London Bridge and organised our wedding suits. On the 17th of August, Brenda's mother Ivy, the two Brendas (Iffland and Greenfield) and Dylys went wedding dress shopping, and as I was to find out later, with excellent results.

The day came, Saturday the 17th of September 1955, which changed my life. Alan, my Best Man and I had gone into Upminster, and I bought Brenda a gold wrist watch, the bracelet of which was in the form of tiny gold leaves. I asked West's the Jewellers for it to be delivered to her that morning before the ceremony, which indeed they did. At this point, I had less than £30 in my bank account, so I was very glad that Brenda's father did not know.

Dylys Davies, Alan Lazell, Me, Brenda, Brenda Stutchbury
© CA Lansley

Our Wedding © Brenda Iffland

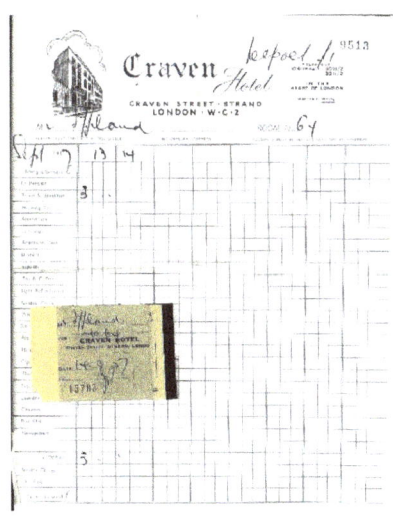

Our wedding night hotel bill © CA Lansley

For our first night together, we stayed at the Craven Hotel, Kings Cross, London, before our rail and ferry travel to Germany. I remember that there was no en suite and the toilet was down on the half landing. It was hilarious when confetti, which had lodged in our clothes, was strewn all down the stairs. It was also a wonderful experience, which I will never forget, to see Brenda for the first time in the bath! So different to the present-day cohabiting! Alan had made all the travel bookings for us, and the next morning, we caught the ferry from Dover before travelling on by train to Frankfurt. Second-class German trains had wooden benches, not upholstered seats as in England! We did not know the location of our Hotel Wuertenburger Hof in the dark, so I asked a taxi to take us, which he did, and after driving around for some time we arrived. In the morning, we saw the station was immediately opposite our hotel; taxi drivers the world over!

Next morning, we caught the train to Hanau expecting to be met by Rudi, but something went amiss. Luckily, I remembered the address as Hindemithe Strasse 48. We were made very welcome by Tante Luise and Rudi, with wonderful home-made cake and coffee. (Tante Luise was the sister of my grandfather Andreas in Hetzbach). As a wedding present, we were given a silver 'Hanauer Rose' sugar spoon. Brenda was also given the traditional wrapped sugar lump 'to give to the Stork.'

On Wednesday the 21ˢᵗ of September, we all visited the Hanau cemetery where my Onkel Wilhelm and 'Grossmutter Hanau' were buried and met an old friend of my uncle. Rudi gave up his bed in the attic for us, which had an enormous feather-filled duvet and we slept very well.

Hotel Friedrich © CA Lansley

We were a little alarmed when the friendly hotel staff opened our luggage and laid out Brenda's nightdress and my pyjamas on the bed! A welcoming which we had never before experienced, until our visit to Crete in 2006 when the so-friendly staff arranged our nightclothes every day in a different comic fashion!

Crete 2006 © CA Lansley

We met so many family members and festivities were held at the Post in Hetzbach, which was run by Onkel Willi and Tante Emmi. This was the favoured location where the wedding parties of many Ifflands had been held, including that of my own parents. On the 26th of September, Onkel Franz brought us to stay with them in Hetzbach and took us to visit the famous Church organ at Amorbach, followed by once again, coffee and cakes, this time at the excellent 'Mühle Café'.

Onkel Franz took us back to Hanau on the 29th and gave Brenda two small diamonds. We still have them, though they have never been set, although it was our intention to do so.

Finally, we caught a train to Ostend, arriving late at Victoria Station on the 1st of October, where Brenda's mother, father and brother Graham met us. We were extremely tired and for the first time (with a ridiculous tinge of guilt!), I slept in her old bed at the family home, 'Bradda' 25 Little Gaynes Lane, Upminster.

Brenda's mother had managed to organise a downstairs furnished flat for us to rent in Forest Gate, after our unsuccessful attempt to rent No.17 Ingrebourne Gardens, the bungalow next door to Alan's parents' house, where we were first offered it, then the offer was withdrawn. 22 Lakehouse Road looked out over Wanstead Flats, a large open area. We started making it into our first home.

For a short time, it became a great meeting point for all our friends (for whom Geoff Davies played the piano in the lounge), and as skiffle was the 'in' music, we all accompanied him on washboards, pots and pans! We still laugh at some of the antics and, of course, Alan's jokes.

Shortly after returning from our honeymoon, Mr Story wrote asking me to return to Iraq for the next phase of the railway survey. Financially, I was obliged to accept. Brenda agreed to this but did not want to be at Lakehouse Road alone, so Brenda (Stutchbury) stayed with her from time to time. My Brenda also stayed with her parents in Upminster, and we still retained the flat. We only had a few more days together.

Me and Mother, taken outside our flat © CA Lansley

15
BACK TO IRAQ AGAIN

On the 11th of October, 24 days after getting married and after spending a distressing pre-departure night at the Normandie Hotel, Knightsbridge, I left London once more to continue a further stage of the Baghdad to Basra railway survey. Mr Tanner, a retired ex-East African Government Surveyor, was in charge of the five-man steam, which included two more retired ex-Government surveyors, Tavener and Lissett, and two workhorse youngsters, Westmacott and myself.

At this time, the weather in Iraq was warm, but as the months passed it became colder and wetter. The survey work was progressing well, with only minor problems, such as when a Sheikh objected to the survey line passing through his date palm plantation, which were solved when an agreed payment was made for trees essentially cut down.

Taking a rest day on Friday, the 21st of October, we visited the 'Ctesiphon,' mentioned in the Bible, the world's largest unsupported arch, which formed part of a palace entrance not far from Nasiriyah.

On the 26th of October, Brenda sent me a photo showing her in her wedding dress (now used as an evening gown) at a dinner held by the Union Castle Line in London and reported in the London Evening Standard. Another letter from Brenda told me that Alan and Dylys had become engaged on the 4th of November and that the event was celebrated by family and friends going to the theatre in London and then out to dinner. This was just before Alan's 21st birthday, which was on the 6th of November.

On the 15th of November, we moved camp to Zubedia. One of our party had brought with him a rifle and on Friday the 25th of November, we went pig shooting in the cotton fields. I am happy to say that we were unsuccessful!

On the 30th, we moved camp to Na'amaniyah and progressed, working back from Kut. The weather was cold, cloudy and with rain seriously affecting the roads. Then on the 17th of December, we moved camp to Kut and continued the measuring and levelling of the route. Unhappily, on the 21st of December, a letter came from my grandfather in England to say that my grandmother Octavia Nina, 'Noni', had died in the morning of the 12th of December.

Christmas Day was just another day. There was nowhere to go and nothing to do, so we all continued working and drank a Scotch or two in the evening. New Year's Day was just the same except that I recorded that we had an excellent turkey dinner.

On the 14th of January 1956, we were up at 5.30 a.m. preparing for our move to Suq where we arrived eventually at 6.15 p.m. The typical ground to be covered was dense date plantations with wide canals and villages in the way, which made it extremely difficult to lay out the survey route. On the 17th, a fire broke out in the nearby reed village, with flames shooting all over the place and ammunition going off, and all the women wailing! Our mode of transport now was mainly by boat, moving along the canals and between the 'floating' reed villages.

On Friday the 20th of January 1956, I once again visited the site of 'Ur of the Chaldees' with one of the survey team. The Ziggurat and Burial Pits of Ur are impressive reminders of the early inhabitants who lived here before 3000 BC. There were wonderfully preserved golden items in the Museum in Baghdad, and I just hope that during the war to oust Saddam Hussein, when looting in Baghdad was rife, these many items from ancient history were not lost. I recalled that when I first came here in February 1954, we found the result of earlier excavations lying on the open ground, consisting of pottery pieces and cuneiform writing but no complete pots.

The railway was to connect Baghdad to Basra, but en route, each local Sheikh wanted the line to pass near his palace. This latest section involved routing the line through the Hammar Lake, a very large expanse of relatively shallow reeds amongst which the traditional Marsh Arabs lived on 'floating' beds of reeds. We could not see directly across the Lake to set out our survey line due to the tall reeds, therefore we set up a theodolite at one end and sent another surveyor by boat to where we intended to head.

There he fired a 'Very' pistol and observed and marked the approximate line so the labourers could cut the reeds and enable us to measure and level across. This procedure was followed until we had cleared the area of reeds. Working in the swamp, the water came over my gumboots and up to the top of my legs and was very cold, in spite of it being a hot day.

On the 7th of February, I recorded surveying in swamp water the whole day among the Marsh Arabs.

Marsh Arabs, me in left foreground © CA Lansley

I am on the far right © *CA Lansley*

The camp then moved to Jeffah. It had taken nineteen cold and painful days to survey through the marsh. I left Jeffah for Baghdad on the 15th of February. While there, I met Alan's father Horace who was on business in Iraq and was also staying at the Sinbad Hotel.

I heard that Mr Story had died of a heart attack on Monday the 20th of February 1956. I felt a personal loss.

16
BACK HOME

On the 1st of March, I flew once more from Baghdad on a BEA 'Viscount' via Amsterdam where I bought Brenda a small pair of silver 'windmill' earrings. Brenda met me as usual at Heathrow. On seeing my grandfather the next day, I noticed just how much older and more tired he appeared, and all were still in mourning for my grandmother.

Opa Goldstein © CA Lansley

After reporting on the 5th to Mr Webb at the office at No. 36 Hall Lane, I took the data, field books, plans, etc., and delivered them to the client in Victoria Street, London.

Since leaving Secretarial Training at Clarks College, Romford, Brenda had been working for the Union Castle shipping line at offices in Fenchurch Street, London. On the 6th of March, I was given a site survey to complete in Warwick. I found local accommodation and Brenda joined me at the weekend, helping me on site as an extra assistant, before catching her train back to Paddington on Sunday afternoon. I had the freedom that, once I had completed the fieldwork and checked the calculations, I could plot the drawings at home. This suited me well and gave my employer many more hours worked in a day.

As a result of working through the marshes of the Hammar Lake for the railway survey in Iraq, all the survey team were advised to contact the Hospital for Tropical Diseases, St. Pancras, London, because of potential infection by 'bilharzia' from the swamps. This I did on the 30th of April 1956, and underwent a very unpleasant but thorough medical examination.

It was at this time that on the 2nd of May, I bought our next form of transport, a brand-new grey Austin A30 van, 648 GPU (£324.10.3) but received £105 off for my old Austin 8 1939. John Greenfield introduced me to someone who very expertly cut out the rear side panels, and inserted glass to make it into an estate car. This was just days before the government regulations changed, preventing this. We were very happy with our first new car.

On the 9th of May, I was admitted to the hospital for Tropical Diseases having found that I had amoebic dysentery. I was treated with 'Emmetine, Bismuth and Iodide' (EBI) for two weeks, making me feel very sick and reducing my heart rate, so I was mostly confined to bed and then had to convalesce for a further two weeks.

However, 'the gang' all enjoyed a really sunny day at Frinton on the 7th of July.

'The Gang' Frinton July 1956 © CA Lansley

Before being taken ill, I had been surveying a large project for Basildon New Town, and on recovering, I continued this until October.

Towards the end of 1956, the Union Castle Shipping Line (where my Brenda worked) held their Annual Dinner and Dance for which she had managed to get tickets for us to go together with John and Brenda Greenfield. It was great fun for us all.

With John and Brenda Greenfield 1956 © CA Lansley

Jean Roger Hardy had invited us to his wedding at Eaubonne, France, and on the 7th of September 1956, we crossed by ferry in our A30, drove until it was dark, and parked up with both Brenda and I sleeping in the back of our van. We were awakened by voices, and on looking out, we saw that we were in the middle of a field! Luckily, the farm workers picking the onions were friendly.

The 8th of September was the wedding, but we were very unsure where to find Eaubonne and its Catholic church, after a night in the field, and virtually unable to speak French. We drove off and more by luck, arrived outside the church as the couple were just entering. Neither of us had experienced a ceremony such as this with people getting up, moving about and talking during the service.

We followed the party to a chateau where long tables had been laid out on the grass in the sun, but we had a suspicion that, although we had received an invitation, they were not really expecting us to arrive, as extra places had to be laid out. In the chateau, Jean's friends had taken much trouble to set out a graphic tableaux of his life and achievements. It was a fine sunny day, the bride and her bridesmaids sat out on the grass, and we were happy to have taken part.

Our Austin A30 van, 648 GPU, in Paris © CA Lansley

We went on to spend an interesting and hair-raising week in and around Paris when our new car's front bumper was demolished by a French woman driving diagonally across us in the Place de la Concorde.

The remainder of the year was spent in England on various surveys, mainly in the south.

Me as Best Man with Geoff Davies at Alan and Dylys'
Wedding 8ᵗʰ May 1957 © CA Lansley

The year 1957 continued normally, but the great event in May was that on the 4th, my old friend Alan married Dylys Davies.

Alan and Dylys Lazell's wedding 1957. Maureen on the left, my Brenda on the right © CA Lansley

We ensured that they had a good send off, by all 'the gang' following them to London, including to the Air Terminal, before they flew off for their honeymoon to Switzerland.

On the 19th of May, I had just completed a survey at the Mersey River when I was asked to see a Mr Osborne of Cementation Company at Albert Embankment, London and to take my passport and vaccination certificate with a view to going out to India to temporarily take over the Durgapur Steelworks Precise Survey Department, as the Englishman who had been in charge had been instantly dismissed for refusing to allow his children to travel on the same school bus as Indian children. I left London on the 27th of May and arrived in Calcutta the following day.

17
MY FIRST TRIP TO INDIA

As I left the plane on transiting at Delhi, I thought it would not be possible for me to work as the heat was stifling, but luckily, I quickly acclimatised. My task was to set out a precise network of stable survey control markers around the huge site and establish primary baselines. I was, of course, familiar with normal land survey tolerances, but here I was expected to measure with low-expansion Invar steel wires, suspended in a catenary, applying tension at both ends, temperature-corrected and screened from lateral wind, to give accuracies to within millimetres. I had never done this before, and all in the searing sun. However, with my surveying textbooks and common sense, it fairly soon became understandable.

At my desk © CA Lansley

I must say that the Indian survey staff were familiar with the equipment and very helpful. Because of the daytime heat, we experimented successfully with night theodolite observations.

Local Survey Staff © CA Lansley

Brenda sent me this picture of her 22nd birthday, which I had to miss. High fashion!

From left: Dylys and Alan Lazell, My Brenda, Brenda, and John Greenfield © CA Lansley

'Monsoon proper' began on the 28th of June, and with the heat and the rain, progress was slow. On the 1st of August, I collected R.G (Dick) Moore from Mondal Railway Station. He was my newly recruited replacement who had come from England to take over the department. I was asked to stay a while to help him become acquainted with the site.

One notable event on site was that on the 15th of August, Indian Independence Day was celebrated with much pomp and ceremony.

I eventually flew from Calcutta's Dum Dum airport at 8 p.m. on the evening of the 7th of September. At the request of Mrs Story, on my way home, I stopped off in Karachi on Sunday the 8th of September, to look up John Craig, an old friend of hers. We enjoyed a pleasant lunch together before I flew off once more.

Once again, as I returned, I stopped off in Frankfurt and was met by Tante Luise and spent the night in Hanau with Rudi before going to Hetzbach and Michelstadt. On Friday the 13th, I left Frankfurt without incident! As ever, Brenda met me.

18
6 BROOKMANS CLOSE

Prior to going away, arrangements had been made for us to purchase a three-bedroom house to be built at 6 Brookmans Close, Cranham, Upminster. It was completed and we moved in on the 31st of November. There was a great deal to do, and as we could not afford carpets, we set to and sanded and varnished the wooden floors. This gave us aching knees, but also great pleasure and satisfaction.

6 Brookmans Close © CA Lansley
Ivy, Brenda and Graham

My brother John's wife, Thea, gave birth to their first son Clifford, on the 12th of December 1957. He was born in Kuala Lumpur where the Army had posted John to RAMC Kowloon.

On the 13th of December 1957, I drove my grandfather (Opa) to Paddington Station from where he was off to visit Christian friends. I said goodbye, not knowing that I would never see him again. He died peacefully on the 6th of April 1958, aged 85, while Brenda and I were in the air on our way to India. He knew that Brenda was expecting a baby, much to his delight.

Late in 1957, Dick Moore had written to me saying that there was too much work on the Durgapur site and asking if I would consider coming back. Subject to bringing Brenda with me, and a negotiated tax-free salary, we agreed to go. This caused great concern for Brenda's parents, who now knew that she was pregnant and feared we were going into the wilds. We were reassured by Cementation that Brenda would have excellent free medical attention. We therefore both agreed this would be a worthwhile experience for us.

19
TO INDIA WITH BRENDA

We flew from London at 11 a.m. on the 5th of April 1958, and it was snowing! Arriving in Calcutta, the temperature was 95°F.[17] Some change! We were met by a Cementation representative and taken to the company guesthouse in Belvedere Road, where we stayed and explored Calcutta a little until the 8th, when we caught the Toofan Express train to Mondal Station near Durgapur.

Our bungalow was not ready, so we temporarily lodged with a senior engineer, Mr Hibbert and his wife. Then Dick Moore and I started work while Brenda and Dick's wife Mary went to stay for ten days with Joe, a friend at Dahnbad. When Brenda returned to our home, Bungalow D8/2, Benachitti, we hired a cook/bearer, 'Tony' and a cleaner, 'Muttiah.' Everything we needed in the way of furnishings and kitchenware was provided free to us by Cementation Patel. The water and electricity supplies had not yet settled down, there were frequent power cuts, and our water had to be delivered by lorry bowser.

On the 19th of June, strong winds heralded the coming monsoon. Brenda would sit outside our bungalow with

---

[17] 35°C

perspiration dripping off her fingers, but she coped wonderfully. Dick Moore was a keen photographer, and in view of the forthcoming birth, suggested that I buy a cine camera to properly record the baby's early days. This I did and bought an 8mm Kodak camera, which was well used, and we have many happy reminders of Claire coming into our lives, as well as of our time in India.

On our third wedding anniversary, we visited the Maithon Dam and took cine films.

Our small side garden with the cleaner 'Muttiah'
© CA Lansley

Time passed, mainly with work, but also weekend lunches, where 'Memsahibs' would compete with each other in the variety and splendour of their curries and side dishes. A bachelor, John Hailwood, organised monthly musical evenings at his bungalow and entertained us with his 'Black Box' record player, playing both classical and popular music, which was immensely enjoyed by everyone. Sitting out in the warm half-light was almost magical.

Brenda with a banana palm in our garden © CA Lansley

Local transport © CA Lansley

Progress on the site was made, and with the odd weekend in Calcutta, we were soon in October 1958.

20
CLAIRE ADELE

On the 19th, Brenda woke me at 3.50 a.m., knowing that the baby was on the way. Our driver, who had been on standby, took us in the Jeep Station Wagon to the hospital at Sanctoria at 5.00 a.m. Brenda went into labour at 11.00 a.m. When I came into the delivery room to see her, she was so occupied and obviously in pain that I could not help her, so I waited outside.

Claire Adele was born at 3.30 p.m., weighing 7lbs. 9oz and was 20 inches long. A nurse brought the baby out from the delivery room and I went in to see Brenda. Then the nurse carried Claire, who was lying in an enamelled dish, and put her on a table outside in the sun. I counted her fingers and toes, and I was a very happy father. I sent cables to the family.

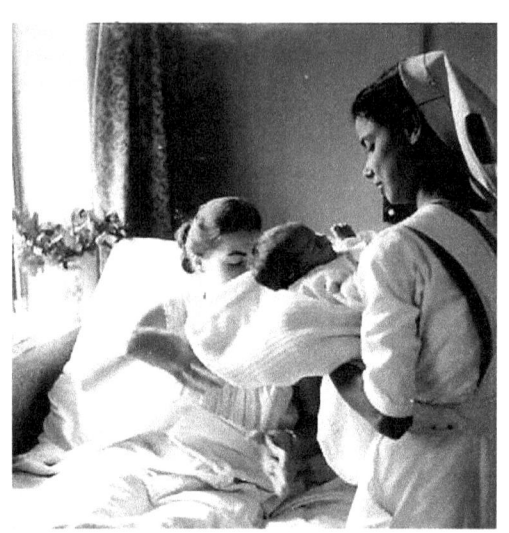

The new arrival © CA Lansley

We were now a family.

Dr. N. C. SEN,
M.S., D.G.O., F.R.C.S., F.I.C.S.
TELEPHONE: ASANSOL 242 & 247
(EXTENSION)

SANCTORIA
DISHERGARH P.O., BURDWAN
(WEST BENGAL)

CLAIRE ADELE IFFLAND,
daughter of Mr.M.W.Iffland and
Mrs.Brenda Joy Iffland was born
in the Sanctoria Hospital, Disergarh
P.O.on the 19th October, 1958 at
3-30 p.m.

(N. C. Sen).

172

Me with Claire © CA Lansley

The survey work on site progressed well in spite of the heat.

Survey © CA Lansley

The Indian Authorities wanted local labour to be used wherever possible, rather than the usual pumping of concrete to the various foundations. This was a much slower alternative, but 'head-pan' men and girls, in a long file, walked up and down the ramps like ants and deposited their load of concrete.

Head pan labour © CA Lansley

In other places, both mothers and their very young children were employed, sitting on the ground, breaking up the local stone, laterite, with hammers for the road's sub-base. At the same time as the British were building a new steelworks in India, German and Russian firms were also building new plants. It could have been foreseen that it was only a matter of time before our UK steel industry would be in jeopardy, with many closures.

On site © CA Lansley

Head pan girl © CA Lansley

Brenda was coping well with feeding Claire. We had ordered a wicker cradle from 'Kingleys,' a cane shop in Asansol, which was our nearest village. The cradle was removable from its stand, which meant that Claire could also be transported in the car, usually a 'Hindustan Traveller' (a Morris built under licence), which is still being made in India today.[18] We had also ordered a full-size mahogany drop-side cot and a playpen. This was made for us by the skilled Sikh carpenters on the site, for which we paid a very reasonable amount, but Claire hated to be isolated in the playpen. We have been delighted that not only have most of our own children and grandchildren used the cradle, but also some of our friends' children. The cradle stands in excellent order, awaiting the next generation which we hope to live to see.[19]

---

[18] The car model was the Hindustan Ambassador built under licence by Hindustan Motors.

[19] My father did, in fact, live to see the cradle used by many of his great-grandchildren, and a family Cradle Book has been produced with photos of the 24 babies who have so far been in it.

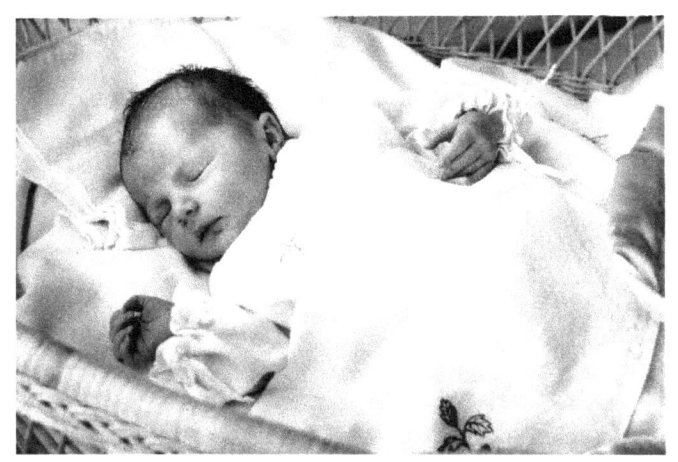

Claire Adele © CA Lansley

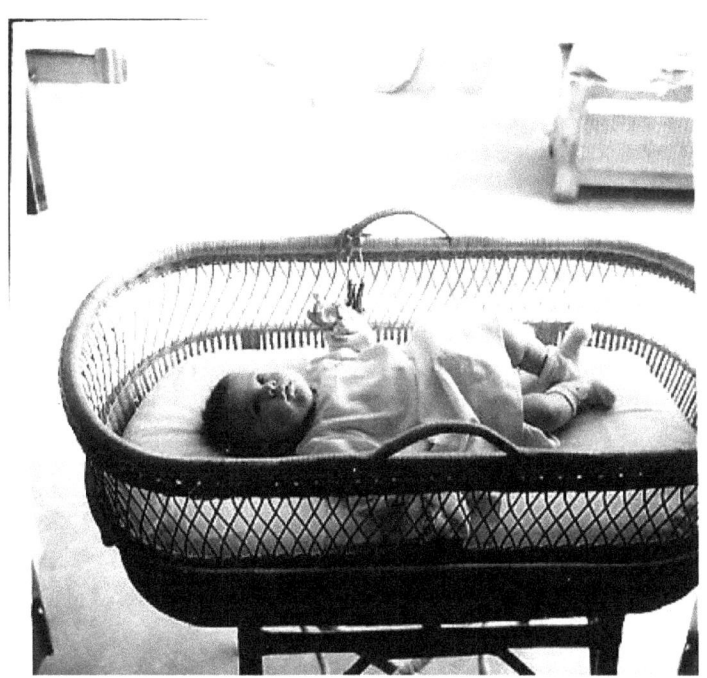

Claire Adele in the wicker cradle © CA Lansley

Rural India is a totally different world from that of England's, with poor peasant farmers trying to water their fields from irrigation ditches and with women, still wearing their saris, up to their waists in the 'tanks' of large muddy ponds which serve the village's needs. But it was all very colourful, exciting, and an experience I was glad to have had.

Fishing © CA Lansley

Claire was now three months old and on Sunday the 25th of January 1959, I took Brenda to show her how the site had developed, with the construction of the blast furnaces. The men were starting to line the inner faces with special oven bricks, and access was gained only by a low opening at the base. For 'posterity', I decided to take Claire inside the furnace with me, but of course, she would never remember this event.

Visiting the blast furnace 25th January 1959 © CA Lansley

At this time, we were planning our return to the UK. We could well have continued for a further tour, if not for the understandable pressure from grandparents eager to see their first grandchild. In reality, Brenda and I also really needed a break.

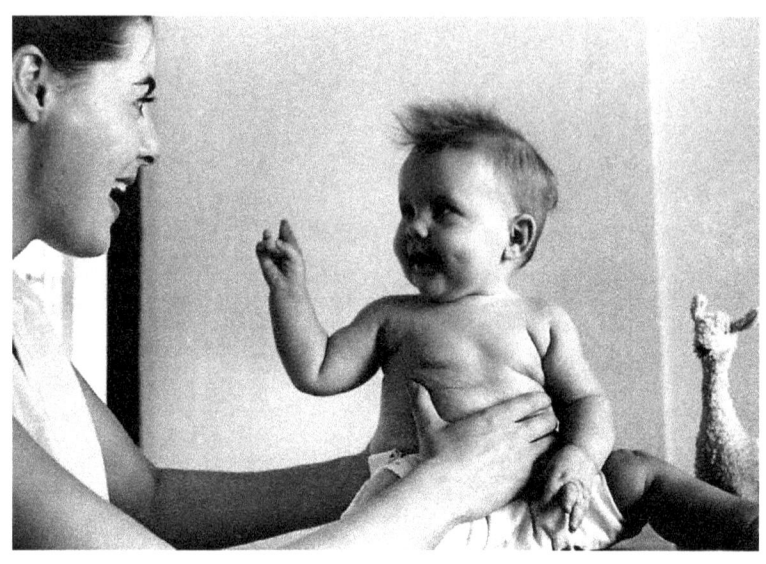

Brenda and Claire with Phooey the giraffe © CA Lansley

We had fun working out our route home. Our first stop was to be Beirut, then onto Rome, Zurich, Frankfurt and finally arriving back home on the 19th of July 1959.

On the 3rd of February, we received our reservations. The Calcutta office had made the bookings for us. We would fly home on the new jet, Comet IV. Our first stopover was to be at the Metropole Hotel in Beirut, followed by the Quirinale Hotel in Rome, and finally, the Hyzes Plaza in Zurich.

On the afternoon of the 3rd of February, the Duke of Edinburgh visited the site and drove around the Steelworks. All the wives and families were in their best clothes, cheering and celebrating this memorable occasion.

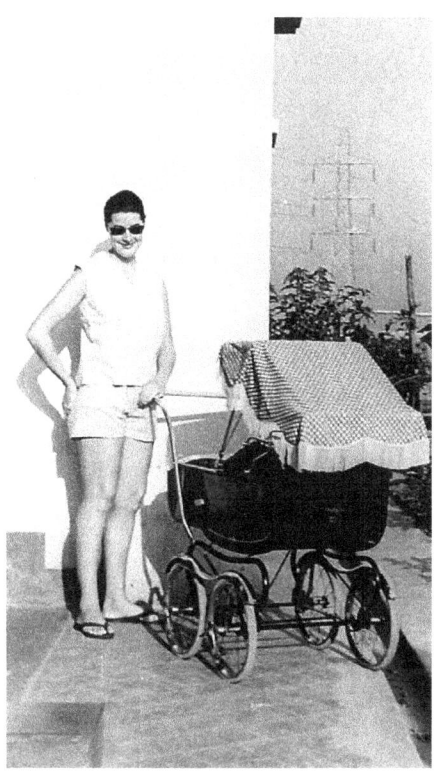

Brenda © CA Lansley

We had arranged that on the 22nd of February 1959, Claire would be christened by the Rev Kenyon Wright at the Methodist Church in Raniganj. All the members of our usual congregation were present. Inside the church was a beam suspended high up from the ceiling, from which a sheet was hanging. This was connected to a rope passing through a hole in the church wall. Coming through the hole outside, it was attached to the *punka wallah's* foot. By him occasionally raising and lowering his foot as he relaxed on the ground, a cool breeze was created inside. Following the service, the Vicar and our friends joined us for a curry lunch at our bungalow.

Rev. Kenyon Wright's card © CA Lansley

On the 29th of May, John, Thea and baby Clifford passed through Dum Dum airport, Calcutta, on their way home from John's Far East posting. We managed an hour and a quarter with them before they flew off. That night, we stayed at the company flat and returned to Durgapur the next day.

The photograph below is from when Thea came to Upminster with baby Clifford, probably in June, and visited Mother and Edgar. They all had tea in the garden at 'Bradda' with Brenda's family, before we returned home.

Left to right: Thea with Clifford, Edgar, Ivy, Ruth, Edmund and Suzanne, the standard poodle © CA Lansley

Our packing case taking our effects, which had been selected to be sent home to the UK © CA Lansley

21
COMING HOME WITH CLAIRE

Then came the day. On Monday the 6th of July, we flew on the new Comet IV from Calcutta to Beirut, the first leg on our way home.

Beirut © CA Lansley

After Durgapur, Beirut was wonderful; sea, moderate sun, and very good food at the Metropole Hotel. We stayed from the 7th until the 9th, and enjoyed playing on the sand with little Claire, but she definitely did not like getting her bottom wet by the waves!

Later on the 9th, we flew on to Rome where we had been booked into the Quirinale Hotel. We were met by white-gloved staff who showed us to our room, a magnificent suite with very elaborate wall coverings that made it difficult to identify the door opening as it all blended in so well. Claire was just beginning to exercise her legs, holding onto the foot of the bed and jumping up and down.

We were late for our meal, but the waiter brought a large trolley loaded with food which we thoroughly enjoyed. Later that day, we found that the room cost was at least four times more than we had expected, and more than the Italian currency that we had brought with us. The next day, we moved to a more modest hotel, but it had been a good experience!

We began exploring the wonderful city of Rome, but with it being July, it was extremely hot and we had not made any allowances for carrying a very heavy baby. After one day's sightseeing, we were almost on our knees, but managed to find a shop where we purchased a lightweight folding pushchair. We then saw all the major sites: the Coliseum, the Sistine Chapel, and the Vatican Square, although the Pope did not appear. (In June of 2006, sister Ursula and her husband Hubert spent a week in Rome, but could not wait in the heat to view the Sistine Chapel as there was a kilometre-long queue! No such problem in 1959.)

Once more on our way back home, we caught a flight to Frankfurt where we had pre-arranged an Opel hire car. We drove to 48 Hindemithstrasse, Hanau, the home of my godfather Wilhelm Jung (who died in June 1954) and his wife Luise (who was a sister of my Hetzbacher grandfather Andreas; therefore, their son Rudolph was in fact my uncle even though he is only one year older than I am!). We were made most welcome by Rudi and his mother. We then travelled onwards to Michelstadt in the Odenwald, where we saw the family and experienced a difficult meeting with Hedwig and little Ursula when they called at Neutorstrasse.[20]

All too soon, we were off on our last leg to Heathrow, to be met by the family on Sunday the 19th of July. The next few weeks were spent taking Claire to meet the family and friends. Such a happy time!

---

[20] The house in Neutorstrasse was, and still is, the family home and travel business of the Wissmüller Family. Lore Wissmüller was my father's first cousin.

22
A SURVEYOR'S LIFE AND THE BIRTH OF JANET ELAINE

On the 24th of August, I restarted work in the UK. Also in that week, pre-arranged work started on building a brick garage and glass extension to the rear of our house in Brookmans Close. The work also included the laying of a turf lawn with invaluable help from Brenda's father, Edmund.

The garden at Brookmans Close © CA Lansley

The hectic routine of surveys in England resumed fairly quickly, until I was called to see Cementation Company in London, where I was asked if I would return to Durgapur for two or three months, but leaving on 3rd October. I was not too keen, and in the event they found another surveyor to go.

Now that I was back in the UK, I needed a car. While in Durgapur, I had received various brochures from home on the latest cars and, after much deliberation, ordered a brand new model, a blue Triumph Herald. While waiting for delivery, I bought an old black Austin VLE233. The new Triumph Herald was delivered on the 25th of November 1959, Registration No.340 JPU.

© CA Lansley

Meanwhile, Edgar had joined J.A. Story & Partners to train as a Land Surveyor in the same way as I had done. However, they decided to send him to a Story site in Nigeria, despite his being an inexperienced young Assistant Surveyor. There, they left him alone with a non-English speaking African, 'dropping him in at the deep end', just as I had been in January 1953 when I was sent to level the breached seawall at Canvey Island. At least the people around me spoke English! For Edgar, it was an extremely difficult posting, both physically and mentally, but he survived! I still have some of his anguished letters written at the time when he was given an outline of what was required and then left alone in the bush with only a Nigerian assistant.

A new steelworks was to be built at Llanwern, Monmouth. In April 1960, I was seconded from J.A. Story & Partners to Engineering Surveys Ltd., another survey firm, which had secured a contract to supply technical staff for the setting out project. ESL had no steelworks-experienced staff, and because of my recent work at Durgapur, I was sent.

One of the massive piled survey pillars which were constructed around the site © CA Lansley

I was booked into the Stow Park Hotel in Newport and was expected to work a complete month before being allowed leave. This was not unusual for a Land Surveyor. However, Brenda was pregnant. We did meet up at Aunt Margaret's (Dadit's) home in Bartestree, Hereford, one weekend at the end of May when Brenda brought Claire to see me.

In June, we took a week's family holiday with Alan, Dylys and baby Philip, travelling down to Studland. Both Dylys and Brenda were very pregnant! Our hotel was very near the beach and adjacent to the well-known 'Old Harry Rocks.' The girls took it easy, and Alan and I entertained the young ones. As ever, a happy time.

Work continued on the steelworks.

Hugh, my Assistant. Blast Furnace in the background.
© CA Lansley

I came home to Upminster for my weekend break on Saturday the 16th of July, and was preparing to return to the site on the Sunday afternoon of the 17th, but Brenda persuaded me to stay until the next morning. Janet Elaine was born at 11.35 p.m. A beautiful girl!

Leave was granted, and I returned to site nine days later. The difficult work at Newport continued, and in mid-September, I was allowed one week's unpaid leave to decorate our house.

Claire © CA Lansley

Thereafter, work continued on site in spite of the bad conditions until, after an eight-hour day had been completed on the 23rd of December, we were allowed to go home. Three days after Christmas leave, Storys asked me to undertake a rapid survey locally before once more returning to Newport. Here, I stayed until the end of January, after which I resumed my full survey duties for JAS.

At the beginning of April 1961, I was briefed to take a survey group to Eskdalemuir, north-east of Dumfries, Scotland (where I stayed at the nearby Crown Hotel, Lockerbie). The client was the Atomic Energy Research Establishment, through Consulting Engineers, and our task was to position and coordinate a series of ground markers where microphones would be buried deep into bedrock, the scheme being called a 'Seismic Array.' These microphones were to be linked to recording devices, with the intention that the widespread use of these units across the moor could pinpoint a distant atomic explosion fairly accurately, and the country from which it came. This was all part of our Cold War defences.

The team were on site for over seven weeks, working in some of the most arduous terrain with mainly bad weather and few roads, resulting in our Land Rovers being stuck daily in the peat and having to locate and pay a farmer to tow us out with his tractor!

Eskdalemuir and a stuck Land Rover © CA Lansley

Survey followed survey at sites all over the UK for Consulting Engineers, Architects, Government bodies and organisations such as the Ford Motor Company. This covered a great diversity of specifications, which were challenging and interesting.

The Triumph Herald 340 SPU, after heavy usage, had been giving major mechanical trouble, so on the 16th of June 1961, I replaced it with a new two-tone Triumph Herald 916 XEV.

*On the way to Brenda's friend Maureen Blade's wedding to
George Travers © CA Lansley*

Alan had constructed a mini catamaran in his house.
Amazingly patient Dylys! This provided much fun for the
children and adults! On our first visit to Greatstone, Kent,
Dylys' brother Geoff came down for the day. Unfortunately,
when Dylys and Brenda tried to get on at the same time, it
sank under their combined weight!

Alan's homemade catamaran.
Front left: Claire, mid-front Janet, right-front Philip Lazell
Behind: Alan, David Lazell, Geoff Davies (standing), Dylys
© CA Lansley

Garden picnic with the Lazells and Greenfields
© CA Lansley

The photo above was taken on our second visit to Greatstone. This garden was not the same as the bungalow on the seaward side of the road, as in 1961, where the bungalow had been virtually on the beach, and sand flowed in through the kitchen door!

23
ONWARD AND UPWARD

By this time, I had gained technical and administrative competence and progressed from Senior Surveyor to Group Leader with emphasis on Architectural Building surveys and large Engineering projects. The main office had relocated to Laurence Pountney Hill, off Cannon Street, in the City of London, while the original Story's office (in their house at 36 Hall Lane, Upminster) was used for administration.

An enquiry had been received from a businessman, Mr Charles Gale from Kuwait, about surveying for the possible construction of a new commercial harbour at Shuiba. Instead of one of the partners flying out, I was asked to go and meet the client and assess the work. Prior to going, I was also asked to meet with Maunsell, Posford and Pavry, the consulting engineers for whom I had worked in Iraq and who were now interested in a scheme for a new power station in Kuwait. However, there was insufficient time to combine both visits. Posfords needed confirmation of the various ground heights at the Power Station site relative to the Kuwait National Survey benchmarks (precisely measured height marks), and I went out later to undertake this task.

On the 18th of September 1962, I met with Mr Gale, studied and photographed the site and made contact with the

British Embassy, Municipality H.Q., and the Secretary of the Development Board of the Public Works Authority. During this first visit, the weather was excessively hot, but fortunately involved mainly short site visits and meetings in various offices, and not actually being out in the sun surveying!

The Gales lived in a comfortable air-conditioned home, with a basement decked out as a bar. At this time, alcohol was allowed by licence for expatriates only, but Fridays were still meant to be dry. Mrs Gale had artistic inclinations, and the large air-conditioned basement room was walled with mirrors on which she had painted nude figures of women in artistic poses. Each Friday, the local Sheikhs would be invited to gather in the basement and enjoy the scenery and forbidden alcohol!

I completed my trip and returned to the UK on the 25th of September. As usual, I was immediately back into more site inspections and quotations after having briefed the Partners on my trip.

On the 9th of October, I was off once more to Kuwait, this time to meet Posford's Peter Rowley, who was the Engineer for the Power Station project. The spirit levelling was to be from known Government height points to specific borehole positions at the intended Power Station, and also to establish site benchmarks for future reference. The work was completed, and I returned and delivered my report to

Posford's office in Victoria Street, London, on the 16th, back in time for Claire's 4th birthday on the 19th of October.

The winter was cold with snow lasting through to February 1963, but once again the Lazell and Iffland families were planning ahead and booked 'Greenlands Cottage,' Goathorn, Studland, for their summer holiday in June.

At Easter in 1963, we took the children to the London Zoo for the first time, which was quite an event in their young lives.

During a busy September in 1963, four of the senior staff entered into discussions with Partner John Webb: Alan Catchpole, John Grant (sadly now deceased), Archie Niven and myself. John Webb's intention was to offer each of us promotion to Associate, so we were encouraged to make a financial commitment to the firm by making loans in £500 units, which would bear interest. At this time, the firm was having significant financial problems. Mr Webb confided in me that the Lloyds Bank Manager described his way of raising funds as being 'ingenious'!

I believe we all took part, but I only put down for one unit (£500). How much was invested by my colleagues I did not know. With my family commitments I could not readily have access to such a sum, but after discussion with Brenda's parents they lent me the amount. This was duly repaid to them with the interest they had foregone in the meantime.

In December 1963, I led a team to survey the Underground railway tunnel from Bank Station to Liverpool Street Station. This involved traversing down the escalators at one station, along the tunnels and up and out at the other end, all at night after the electricity had been switched off. The link would be made on the surface by running a connecting traverse. The purpose was to measure precisely where the London Stock Exchange was located on the surface in relation to the nearest face of the Underground tunnel so that driving piles for the proposed new Stock Exchange structure would not cause havoc. Great care had to be taken to make all the necessary corrections, such as temperature, as above ground at night it was freezing but in the tunnels it was 70°F. The below-ground angle and distance circuit closing directly with the surface traverse meant that it was possible to mathematically prove its accuracy. The main problem, apart from the very dirty conditions in the tunnels, was that we could only work at night when the current was switched off. We arrived and prepared to work on the surface from 9 p.m. After about 1 a.m., we were permitted into the tunnel. However, we had to be off the tracks before 3 a.m. approximately, as the current would be reconnected. The fieldwork was completed in early January after careful field checks.

January the 7th 1964 was Claire's first day at school. Oglethorpe Primary School was definitely not to her liking, and she did not want Brenda to leave her. She was very tearful, bringing back memories of my first visit to school in Michelstadt.

Electricity Board Engineers had noted that the legs of the major pylon on the north bank of the River Tyne near Wallsend were deforming as the structure appeared to be gradually slipping down the riverbank. Since September 1963, I had been travelling up with my assistant to assess and establish the survey control to detect any movement or settlement, before remedial action could be taken.

Wallsend pylon, River Tyne © *CA Lansley*

These readings were taken, staying for about one week each time, initially at two weekly intervals, then at monthly intervals for over a year, though latterly I could complete the measurements more rapidly. This routine was fitted in between my other commitments, even when we were on holiday with Alan and Dylys at a farmhouse by the Toll Road at Goatshorn.

This was the main pylon on the north bank of the Tyne, with high cables spanning the wide river to a similar pylon located on the south bank. © CA Lansley

The engineering assistant showed no fear as he walked across to me as I took readings on the steel trusses. I moved about on my bottom!

On the 21st of January, I was forced to stay overnight in Doncaster due to dense fog almost all the way north, continuing my journey the next morning when the fog had lifted. Fortunately, we no longer have to experience these 'pea-soupers,' thanks to the Clean Air Act.

It was bitterly cold. © CA Lansley

24

THE ARRIVAL OF PETER GRAHAME MARK

Brenda was pregnant for the third time. The baby was expected in early summer, and I had been to the London office in my car when I was hit by a van owned by the City Window Cleaning Company on Thursday the 4th of June, which damaged my front offside wing. Luckily, I got all the driver's details and successfully claimed for the damaged front wing.

The damaged wing was quickly forgotten as on Saturday the 6th of June 1964, at 6.25 a.m., weighing 7lbs. 12oz, Brenda gave birth to our son, Peter Grahame Mark, a brother for Claire and Janet. Our family was complete. The next day was Brenda's 29th birthday and a double celebration.

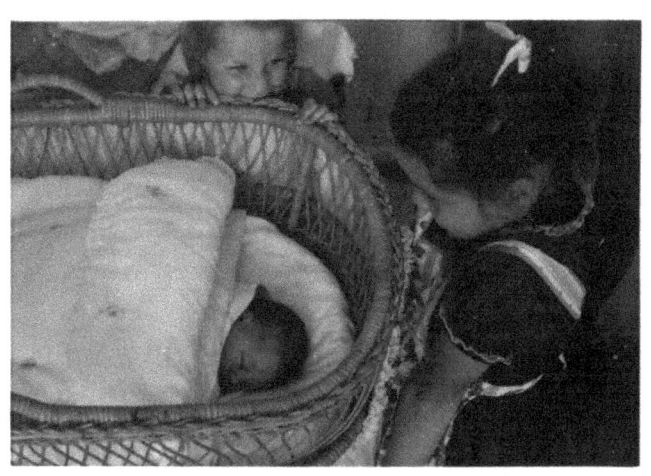

Peter Grahame Mark with Claire and Janet © CA Lansley

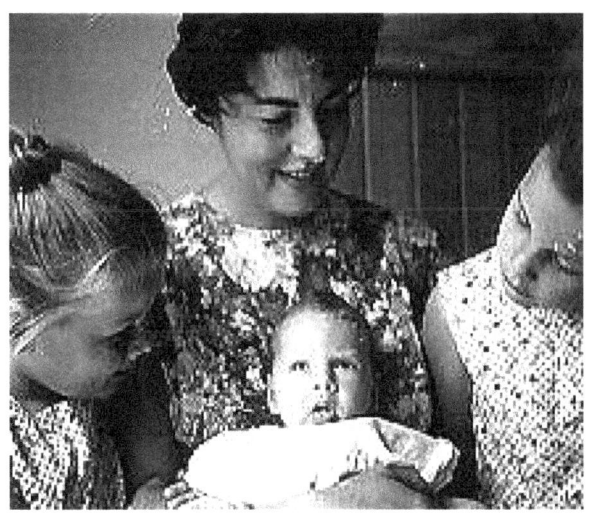

Left to right: Janet, Brenda with Peter, Claire © CA Lansley

In the garden at Brookmans Close. Claire is in the
foreground, Janet is on the slide and Peter is in the pram.
© CA Lansley

Left to right: Claire, Brenda with Peter, Janet and me
© CA Lansley

This chronicles the first thirty-two years of my life.

THE LATER YEARS OF MARTYN IFFLAND

This has been the story of my father's life up to the age of 32. By this age, he had been married for 9 years, had had a mortgage for 5 years and had 3 children. I suspect that he became unable to continue his writing around the age of 80 because of failing eyesight.

In 1970, at the age of 38, he and my mother decided that they needed a bigger house. They bought a house in Courtenay Gardens, Upminster, which was directly opposite their best friends Alan and Dylys Lazell, who lived there with their four boys. He lived in the same house for the rest of his life.

At the same time as moving house, he started his own business, Iffland and Associates, in partnership with his brother Edgar. For a time, he ran the business from the house before moving into premises in Upminster. While bringing up three children, my mother also provided secretarial and bookkeeping support for the business over many years.

In the 1970s, my father joined the DVW e.V., the German Association for Geodesy, Geoinformation and Land Management, and undertook some survey work in Berlin. Through this organisation, my parents met Hans and Gisela

Kothe, who lived in Wiesbaden, Germany, and they became significant life-long friends.

My father remained a Land and Engineering Surveyor until his retirement in 1997. He was a Director of the Guild of Incorporated Surveyors and of the UK Land and Hydrographic Survey Association Ltd. He was a founder member of The Survey Association of which he became first a Committee Chairman, then Vice President and finally President from 1994-1997.

As a teenager, I well recall our first family visit to Michelstadt in Germany where we met family members. My father's first cousin Lore Wissmüller (the daughter of his father's brother Karl), her husband Reinhard and her extended family made us so welcome.[21] Through our father, we established a relationship with Tante Lore and the German family which still continues. We have subsequently visited Michelstadt on a number of occasions. German family members have also visited us in Upminster. My father said in a speech that he gave to a family gathering in Germany in 2014, that in his soul he was German, and he thanked England for accepting him during very difficult days. He also recalled (at that time) almost 6 decades of happy marriage to our mother and the blessing of his three children.

---

[21] Lore Wissmüller (1932-2024), Reinhard Wissmüller (1931-2004).

In addition to his three children, he had seven grandchildren and, at the time of his death in 2022, eleven great-grandchildren. He saw all of these family members during the last six months of his life, which brought him great pleasure. What he wanted probably more than anything else in life was to have my mother by his side and to be in touch with and surrounded by his family.

I hope that by publishing his story, his memory will live on. It might also be of interest to those currently working in the world of Land Survey to see just how much has changed.

~ Claire Adele Lansley, née Iffland

My mother's 60th birthday in June 1995 with my father, children, spouses and grandchildren

Rear left to right: Henry Holden, Jan Holden, Neil Holden, Martyn Iffland, Charles Lansley, Peter Iffland

Mid left to right: Bryony Holden, Emily Holden, Tara Iffland, Claire Lansley, William Lansley on lap, Susan Iffland

Front: Charlie Holden, Brenda Iffland, Charlotte Lansley

© CA Lansley

My father with his cousin, Lore Wissmüller, 2014
© CA Lansley

www.ingramcontent.com/pod-product-compliance
Lightning Source LLC
Chambersburg PA
CBHW051305120626
46547CB00015B/2089